Let's begin a self-reflection journey to greater happiness and equanimity

JAIN PATH

Supported by JAINA's
Long Range Planning Committee

Dr. Manoj Jain

CONTENTS

Introduction ... vi

Jain Philosophy ... 3
    Theory of Life ... 6
    Theory of Soul ... 10
    Theory of Karma ... 15
    Theory of Moksha ... 31

Jain Principles ... 35
    Ahimsa - Nonviolence ... 38
    Anekantavada - Nonabsolutism ... 52
    Aparigraha - Nonpossessiveness ... 64

Core Jain Practices ... 71
    Nonviolence Practices ... 74
    Nonabsolutist Practices ... 84
    Nonpossessiveness Practices ... 94

HASSE - Elements of Happiness ... 103

Conclusion ... 117

Selected Readings from the Tattvartha Sutra ... 121

DEDICATION

This book is dedicated to my parents, Dr. Vinay and Laxmi Jain of Boston and Indore (MP), for their unwavering commitment to Jainism and their profound influence on me in shaping my understanding of this ancient tradition. I am immensely grateful to them for their respect, appreciation, and boundless patience towards me, especially during my exploration of Jainism through a modern lens.

Thanks to JAINA's Long Range Planning Committee:

Chintan Shah (Chair), Yogesh Bafna, Dipak Doshi, Sonia Gehlani, Praful Giriya, Dipak Jain, Manoj Jain, Prem Jain, Sushil Jain, Yogendra Jain, Manish Mehta, Jaina Parekh, Bipin Shah, Jayesh Shah, Mayur Shah, Soha Shah.

Special thanks to Yogendra Jain, Sunita Jain, Pavan Zaveri, Edwin Rodrigues (EC Digital Services), Vithika Badjatia, Pragati Jain, and Darshana Jain.

This book is available online at www.JainPath.org. The ideas presented in this book are available to all, with a humble request for acknowledgement when presented.

Second Edition.

ISBN 978-0-9773178-6-8

Copyright © 2024 Dr. Manoj Jain / Memphis, TN USA.

FOREWORD

Our ancestors have been practicing Jain religion for millennia. Over this time, Jain philosophy and principles have not changed, but the application and practice of religion have changed. Hence, I felt an explanation of Jain philosophy and principles in the context of modern world practices was needed for a new generation.

Jain Path explains Jain religion and philosophy for the modern 21st-century world. In my early upbringing with my grandparents in India, I learned and lived traditional Jainism: daily temple visits, *pooja*, and *kalash* (ablution). In contrast, over the past half-century, with my parents, I have lived and practiced Jainism in America: Spiritual dinner conversations, Sunday temple visits, and JAINA Convention presentations.

The Jain Path is a synthesis of my life experience and my understanding of Jainism and how to take our religion forward. The Jain Path is ideal for both Jains and people of non-Jain backgrounds worldwide. Also, it can serve as a first book to read for non-Jains in mixed marriages or those who are exploring alternate spiritual paths.

The evolution of the Jain Path has taken decades. It was in the summer of 1992 when Dr. Nathmal Tatia, the research director of Jain Vishva Bharati, from Ladnun, Rajasthan, came to Harvard Divinity School as a visiting scholar to write the translation of *Tattvartha Sutra* for the Sacred Literature Series. As our karma would have it, I met him when my parents visited him. I was mesmerized by his scholarliness as well as the ceiling-high stacks of reference books in his living room. Here, Dr. Tatia formulated the central theme of Jainism and the *Tattvartha Sutra* as *Ahimsa-Anekantavada-Aparigraha*, better known as the Triple A's of Jain principles.

Then, in 2007, the Jain Way of Life book developed and designed by Yogendra and Preeti Jain showed that there was a great need to describe how we could bring Jainism into our day-to-day lives. Then, in the summer of 2016, I delivered a presentation on Jainism simplified at the Young Jains of America convention in Los Angeles. Here the 4 T's: Theory of Life, Theory of Soul, Theory of Karma, and Theory of Moksha came to light. In brief, they encompassed the *Tattva* and the *Dravyas*. Also, what became clear to me was our goal in life: happiness, equanimity, and moksha.

Then, during the pandemic years 2020-2022, when we sought to find meaning in our existence and searched for wholeness and completeness, the idea of 24 practices came to be. An idea struck that we can explain Jainism and Happiness in a simple form as present happiness (joy and pleasure), lasting happiness (contentment and equanimity), and eternal happiness (bliss and moksha) as well as with the acronym of HASSE (Health, Affection, Security, Significance and Equanimity).

After the draft of the Jain Path book was complete, we test-piloted the idea with small focus groups in Arihant Academy classes in the spring of 2023. Finally, in the summer of 2023, JAINA's Long Range Planning Committee successfully scaled up sharing the material in collaboration with Jain centers in Boston, Atlanta, New Jersey, New York and Los Angeles.

The Jain Path is evolving. It is a work in progress and needs your input. Jainism will evolve over the next centuries and millennia, but at this moment in time, we want to pause and recognize that Jainism has a splendid history and a spectacular future with its many treasures. We must cherish and preserve Jainism.

Thank you.
Manoj Jain, July 2024
mjainmd1@gmail.com
www.mjainmd.com
+1 901-240-2602
Memphis, TN USA

INTRODUCTION

What is the Jain Path?

When it comes to Jainism it is not merely a religion, but a way of life. Backed by the power of ancient philosophy and universal principles, Jainism is a simple yet powerful daily practice that leads to greater happiness in life via the route of maintaining a state of equanimity.

Followers of Jainism practice a core philosophy of self-effort towards respecting all life forms. Jains believe in the concepts of soul (*atma* आत्मा), *karma* (कर्म), and *moksha* (मोक्ष). Jain philosophy firmly establishes the three central principles of *ahimsa* (अहिंसा) or nonviolence, *Anekantavada* (अनेकांतवाद) or Nonabsolutism, and *Aparigraha* (अपरिग्रह) or Nonpossessiveness. In layman's words, this literally means love, respect and sharing. When we actualize these principles in our daily lives, they lead to core practices such as vegetarianism/veganism, compassion, forgiveness, meditation, open-mindedness, as well as an overall and wholesome concern for the environment and the world that we live in.

Jain Path takes us forward to a happy, healthy, and compassionate life. Walking on the path of Jainism forges us to follow the core principles of love, respect, and sharing coupled with strong faith, right knowledge, and disciplined conduct (*Samyak Darshan* सम्यक दर्शन, *Samyak Gyan* सम्यक ज्ञान, and *Samyak Charitra* सम्यक चारित्र). For Jains, happiness is not a fleeting pleasure, rather it is equanimity with contentment and harmony with all living beings.

The Jain Path book takes us through a journey of simplifying, recategorizing, and reframing our religion for modern times. There are the 3 P's, 4 T's, 3 A's and 24 Practices. The three P's are Philosophy, Principles, and Practices. The 4 T's are Jain Philosophy with the Theory of Life, Theory of Soul, Theory of Karma, and Theory of Moksha. The 3 A's are the principles of Ahimsa, *Anekantavada*, and *Aparigraha*, and the 24 Practices, much like the 24 *Tirthankaras*, are Vegetarian/Vegan/Jain Diet, Forgiveness, Compassion, Service, Yoga/Exercise, Carefulness, Intoxicant Free, Stress-Free, Open-Mindedness, Meditation/Mindfulness, Respect, Humility, Straight-Forwardness, Scripture Reading, Equity, Prayer, Balancing Needs and Wants, Contentment, Fasting, Austerities, Controlling Sensual Desires, Art of Dying, Charity, and Environmentalism. All this is derived from our scripture, *Tattvartha Sutra*.

In Jainism, our goal in life is to be Happy. Present Happiness is pleasure and joy. Lasting Happiness is Equanimity. Eternal Happiness is Moksha. The ancient scripture, *Tattvartha Sutra*, provides us with guidance, and the Jain Path provides us with the modern day-to-day path.

In our daily life as we strive for happiness, we need to avoid hurting and harming others as well as promote helping others. This process helps us achieve Health, Affection, Security (physical and financial), Significance (purpose in life), and Equanimity. Equanimity, in our lifetime, is to be tranquil and calm without the rollercoaster of sorrows and over-joyousness. *Moksha*, in our multiple lifetimes, is the self-realization of the soul and eternal happiness.

JAIN PHILOSOPHY

 THEORY OF LIFE

 THEORY OF SOUL

 THEORY OF KARMA

 THEORY OF MOKSHA

JAIN PHILOSOPHY

One may wonder about the origins and the evolution of Jain philosophy from ancient to recent times. Historically, the origins of Jainism are rooted in the *Sramana* tradition over 2,500 years ago. The ancient caves have statues similar to present-day statues of *Tirthankars* sitting in a meditative pose. Back in those times, society was based on nonviolence, agriculture, and vegetarianism. Over time, these philosophies, principles, practices, and rituals have ripened and established a concrete place for themselves in Jainism. For example, at the time of Mahavira, no one spoke for and about the *Namokar Mantra*, yet over time, Jain sages realized the path to self-realization was to pay respect to the perfect souls and teachers (*arahants* अरिहंत, *siddhas* सिद्ध, *sadhus* साधू). To this day, Jain philosophy and practices continue to evolve.

Jainism's vast and ancient philosophy is absolutely distinct from that of Hinduism and Buddhism, with the central ideas of Theory of Life, Theory of Soul, Theory of *Karma* (कर्म), and Theory of *Moksha* (मोक्ष). From these four theories come three core principles, so-called AAA - *Ahimsa* (अहिंसा), *Anekantavada* (अनेकांतवाद), *Aparigraha* (अपरिग्रह). And from these principles come core daily practices such as 1. Vegetarian/Vegan/Jain Diet 2. Yoga/Exercise 3. Forgiveness 4. Compassion 5. Respect 6. Open-Mindedness 7. Meditation/Mindfulness 8. Balancing consumerism 9. Living and letting go 10. Environmentalism.

Jain Way of Life is having a belief and enlightened knowledge of Jain philosophy and the principles, and spiritual conduct with the practices.

Any philosophical journey begins with some basic questions. Jain philosophy provides simple-to-understand and easy-to-apply answers:

Who Am I? -- I am the soul, but in our day-to-day lives, the I is much more complicated and expansive.

The ***I is: : I = Self + Me + My + Us + Our***.

I is SELF: the soul and the consciousness or awareness.

I is ME: the body and mind.

However, there's more to "I"

Jain Path

I is MY - emotions, habits, behaviors, and possessions. It is the anger, ego, deceit, and greed we harbor, as well as forgiveness, modesty, straightforwardness, and generosity. The house, the scooter, the car, the smartphone, the saris and kurtas, and the money, all our possessions, are part of MY.

I is US - the spouse, parents, siblings, extended family and friends, and even strangers we share this world with. It is the relationships that tie us to the world.

I is OUR - the city, the nation, the environment, the world, the universe we live in.

So

I = *Self* (soul) + *Me* (mind/body) + *My* (emotions/possessions- anger, money) + *Us* (family, friends) + *Our* (world)

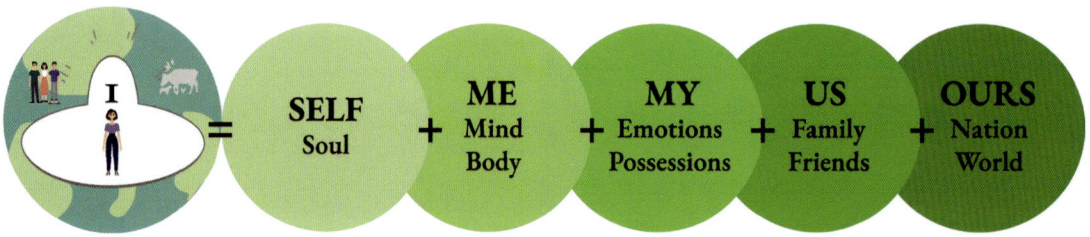

I is Self, Me, My, Us and Ours

When we speak of the I, we need to become aware of which "I" is speaking. Is it the spiritual self, the soul? Or is the I the body and mind which is deeply attached to possessions and materials?

Where did I come from? My soul has been evolving from time infinity, being impacted by past karmic influences.

Why am I here? I am here to realize that "I" am the Soul. The other parts of the I, which are my body, mind, family, friends, possessions, and the world, will help me in this journey. The purpose of I, is to serve others around me. The Jain adage from *Tattvartha Sutra 5.21* is "*Parasparopagraho Jivanam.* - Souls render service to one another."

What is the goal? Jain Way of Life through the AAA-*Ahimsa* (अहिंसा), *Anekantavada* (अनेकांतवाद), *Aparigraha* (अपरिग्रह) provides a four-tier goal to those walking the path of Jainism.

First, we wish to avoid pain and discomfort to ourselves and those around us.

Second, we seek present happiness, which is initially pleasure and temporary, like the sweet taste of chocolate, the smell of a rose, or the satisfaction of helping a child read and graduate from college.

Third, we want lasting happiness, which is contentment or equanimity where we have no aversions or attachments. This resembles a pendulum that stops oscillating widely between sorrowful and joyful moods.

Fourth, we realize that our life is not one lifetime but a continuum of many lives, and we seek moksha as a state of complete and ultimate omniscience and bliss.

हिंसाऽनृतस्तेयाब्रह्मापरिग्रहेभ्यो विरतिव्रतम् ॥ ७.१ ॥

hiṃsā'nṛtasteyābrahmaparigrahebhyo virativratam ॥ 7.1

Abstinence from violence, falsehood, stealing, carnality, and possessiveness - these are the vows

-Tattvarth Sutra

THEORY OF LIFE

Jainism defines the Theory of Life in accordance with its own set of systems and beliefs. The Theory of Life is derived from the six *dravyas* or substances, which are at the core of Jain philosophy.

Theory of Life: Jain philosophy divides the universe into two fundamental units: *Jiv* (living जीव) and *ajiv* (non-living अजीव). Likewise, science divides the universe into living and non-living. Biology is the study of life, and Chemistry is the study of matter. In Jainism, the non-living are further divided by medium of motion and rest like the study of Physics. Both Jainism and science detail the nature of Space and Time as entities that are eternal and continuously undergoing change where nothing is lost or destroyed. This comprises the physical reality in Jainism, paralleling scientific classification. The method of categorizing the universe between *jiv-ajiv* (living and non-living) is critical in providing the Jain and the scientific worldview. In contrast, Western traditions classify the universe differently, as God and non-God.

In Jainism, living beings are further divided on the basis of mobility as Immobile and Mobile beings. Immobile beings are dominated by one sense, whereas mobile are 2-5 sense beings. In science, likewise, classification follows a structure of life, domain, kingdom, phylum, class, order, family, genus, and species. The classification at the level of Life, if living, at the level of Domain is one cell or multiple cells, at the level of Kingdom, is self-mobility or immobile. With fossil evidence, the theory of evolution, and advanced technology, science has further classified life in greater detail. All this classifies the physical reality of living beings.

LIFE
Life
Biologic process such as DNA material

DOMAIN
Eukarya
Multicellular organisms with nucleus containing genetic material

KINGDOM
Animals
Organisms also to move on their own

PHYLUM
Chordates
Animals with a backbone

CLASS
Mammals
Chordates with fur or hair and milk glands

ORDER
Primates
Mammals with collar bones and grasping fingers

FAMILY
Hominids
Primates with relatively flat face and three-dimensional vision

GENUS
Homo
Hominids with upright postures and large brains

SPECIES
Homo Sapiens
Members of the genus homo with a high forehead and thin skull bones

Classification of Life according to science

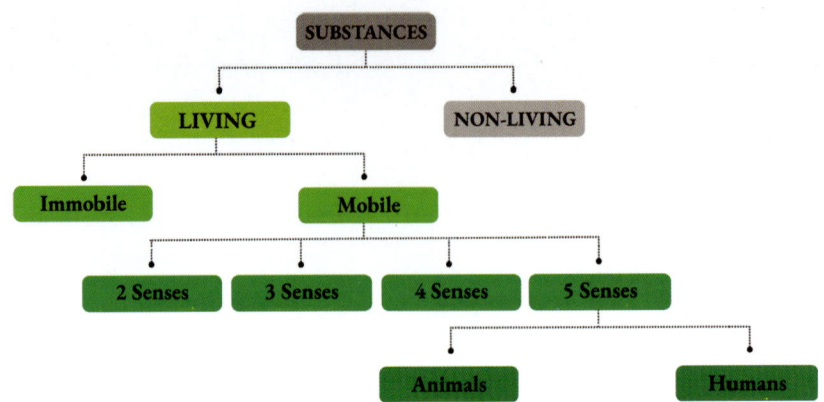

Classification of Life according to Jain philosophy

Jainism classifies non-living in further detail as matter, medium of motion and rest, space, and time.

Matter - *Pudgal* (पुद्गल): In Jainism, matter is made from joining and disintegrating, much like a chemical reaction. Matter or *pudgal* is constituted of atoms (*parmanu* परमाणु). In Chemistry, substances are classified by physical state as gas, liquid, or solid, or their composition elements such as compounds or mixtures. For both Jainism and Science, Matter (non-living) is absolutely distinct from life (living).

Medium of Motion - *Dharmastikaya* (धर्मास्तिकाय): The medium of motion is the instrument in which matter and non-matter make movement. For example, a fish (living creature) moves through water (non-living), where water is the medium of motion. Ether, as identified by today's science, resembles the *Dharmastikaya*.

Medium of Rest - *Adharmastikaya* (अधर्मास्तिकाय): The medium of rest is the instrument in which matter and non-matter rest. If this medium did not exist, then the soul and matter would always be in motion. For example, the shade of a tree provides a place for rest. No clear analogy to *Adharmastikaya* comes in science. However, the study of motion and rest are fundamental to Physics.

Space - *Akash* (आकाश): Traditional Jainism has an extensive explanation of Jain cosmology and the universe. There are detailed descriptions of the present universe, *lokakash* (लोकाकाश), and a universe beyond *alokakash* (अलोकाकाश). There are regions with heavenly and hellish bodies. While no scientific evidence or logic supports such a universe, religious scholars who study Jain cosmology point to the advanced thinking and mathematical knowledge of ancient sages who made an effort to explain the universe in their context. We need to take these explanations of the Jain universe figuratively and not literally. What Jainism and science have in common in relation to space is that they both believe in its infiniteness and beginninglessness.

Time: *(Kal* काल*)* Traditional Jainism goes into great depth in explaining time, which is defined as a measure of change. This continuous and infinite change in the soul and matter is called *Paryaya* (पर्याय). While science and Jainism believe that time is infinite with no clear start or end, Jainism also believes that time is infinite but consists of cycles of ascension and regression with levels of varying happiness and unhappiness. The cycles, figuratively, exemplify the fleeting and universal nature of happiness and unhappiness in the universe over time.

TRADITIONAL	MODERN JAIN WAY OF LIFE

6 Dravyas
Jiv जीव (*life*)
Pudgal पुद्गल (*matter*)
Dharma धर्मास्तिकाय (*motion*)
Adharma अधर्मास्तिकाय (*rest*)
Akash आकाश (*space*)
Kaal काल (*time*)
	Theory of Life
	  Biology
	  Chemistry
	  Physics
	  Space
	  Time

Tattva (*fundamentals*) Jiv तत्त्व vs. Ajiv जीव	Theory of Soul
Asrav (*inflow*), Bandha (*bondage*) Punya (*meritorious*), Pap (*demeritorious*) Samvaar (*stoppage*), Nirjara (*shedding*)	Theory of Karma
Moksha	Theory of Moksha

Jainism and science coincide in their categorization of the physical reality (matter, medium of motion and rest, space and time). But it is only Jainism that then further classifies the metaphysical reality, which includes the theory of soul, theory of karma, and theory of moksha described in Jain *tattvas* (तत्त्व). A side-by-side comparison of traditional Jain philosophy and modern Jain Way of Life philosophy is crucial and helpful in clearly understanding these concepts thoroughly.

THEORY OF SOUL

The Theory of Soul is derived from the first *tattva* (तत्त्व): *Jiv* (जीव) - a living being.

Theory of Soul: Jains believe that each living being is an integration of Soul (*atma* आत्मा) and Body. The Soul is an eternal non-material entity, which, upon death, takes re-birth and continues the cycle of life and death until liberation. Whereas death is defined as the separation of the Soul from its current body, until the Soul achieves liberation and adopts another body, which is called rebirth. The Soul remains the same, yet the body changes. Liberation is achieved only after the Soul frees itself of all karmic influences of the present and past lives.

Science has yet to discover the Soul, yet it was not long ago that science was unaware that plants have life. It was in May 1901 Jagdish Chandra Bose proved that plants, like other living beings, have a life cycle reproductive system and are aware of their surroundings. The scientific method is only several hundred years old, while spiritual methods have been present for over 2500 years.

As spiritual beings, we cannot wait for the scientific discovery of the Soul, which may be decades or centuries away. With faith, we can realize and experience our whole physical and spiritual potential. For some, faith or belief in the Soul (much like the belief in God in other religions) is complex and unsettling. However, our individual spiritual experiences, such as a deeply meditative experience, validate the existence of our Soul, spirit, or consciousness.

It is important to note that it is in the belief of the Soul (or belief in God) where religion and science diverge. Once one accepts the existence of the Soul, or the possible existence of the Soul, then the spiritual journey and understanding of Jain philosophy, principles, and practices can continue. However, even if one does not have faith in the existence of the Soul, even then, the Jain Way of Life as a path to happiness and equanimity provides practical life lessons.

To have an even better understanding of the soul, we need to know its essential attributes and qualities. Jainism provides 15 key attributes and four qualities to give us a deeper and clearer understanding of the soul. Often, it is easier to describe the Soul by what it is not, such as invisible or ego-free, as opposed to what it is.

PHYSICAL	MENTAL	METAPHYSICAL
Indestructible (*avinaashi* अविनाशी)	Desire Free (*nirichchhak* निरिच्छक)	Immortal (*amar* अमर)
Genderless (*alingi* अलिंगी)	Ego Free (*nirvikalp* निर्विकल्प)	Pure (*nirmal* निर्मल)
Ageless (*ajar* अजर)	Alone (*asang* असंग)	Eternal (*nitya* नित्य)
Impenetrable (*abhedya* अभेद्य)	Thought Free (*nirvicharr* निर्विचार)	
Invisible (*aroopi* अरूपी)	Possession Free (*aparigrahi* अपरिग्रही)	
Unbreakable (*akhand* अखंडी)		
Uncapturable (*abadhha* अबद्ध)		
Intangible (*amoort* अमूर्त)		

If someone asks, "What are the qualities of the soul"? The answer to that would be that the soul has four qualities that distinguish it from all other material and non-material things existing in the universe. These qualities are

1. To be aware
2. To have knowledge
3. To have energy
4. To experience bliss

Perception awareness and consciousness - *Darshan* (दर्शन): The soul is blessed innately and inherently to be aware, to perceive, and to be conscious. When we ask the question, "Who am I?" the entity that is asking is not the body, not the mind, but it is the soul. The soul is consciousness and perception. Consciousness allows the soul to be the knower and have cognition. The Soul is manifold, it is awareness, perception, and knowledge. It involves being aware to perceive and to comprehend what is perceived.

Knowledge - *Gyan* (ज्ञान): The soul has the ability to have knowledge. Knowledge is knowing cause-effect relationships along with the ability to comprehend what is perceived. When we recognize that one cigarette puts thousands of tar particles in our lungs, which leads to one cell becoming abnormal and cancerous, we then see how packs of cigarettes over the years lead to fatal lung cancer. Similarly, understanding the impact of every such action in every living individual is infinite knowledge, and this infinite ability is the capacity of the soul.

Energy - *Virya* (वीर्य): The soul has energy to power the body, just like the electricity that powers a lightbulb or a computer. The difference between a corpse and a living person is the energy that the soul provides, which is nothing but the energy of life. Science still has yet to discover this energy, however doctors and scientists know of its existence. A body can have a ventilator pumping air, and an artificial heart pumping blood, and yet the person is dead. What's the difference? The dead person lacks the energy that the soul possesses.

Blissfulness - *Sukh* (सुख): The soul has the quality to experience blissfulness. There is an experience beyond pleasure, beyond happiness, beyond tranquility, contentment, and equanimity. It is oneness and infiniteness, all at the same time.

All these qualities are experienced by all of us in limited measures, but as the soul becomes pure with the practice of self-awareness, self-realization, meditation, and austerities, it then experiences infinite perception - *anant darshan* (अनंत दर्शन) (awareness), infinite knowledge - *anant jnana* (अनंत ज्ञान)(all cause-effect relationships), infinite energy - *anant virya* (अनंत वीर्य) (power that gives vitality to life), infinite bliss - *anant sukh* (अनंत सुख) (equanimity with oneness and wholeness).

The concept of the soul and its well-defined qualities is the contribution of Jain spirituality over day-to-day materialism. This is where the goal for life satisfaction lies, beyond the physical. It is life, realized and experienced, in the metaphysical realm.

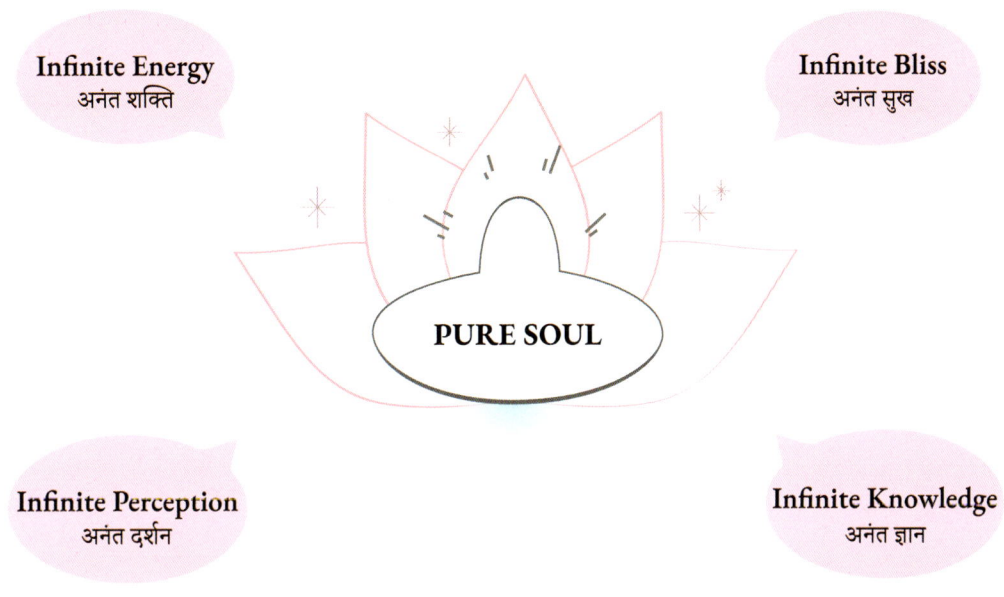

Qualities of Soul

Concept of God in Jainism

One cannot speak of religion without speaking of God. In Jainism, purified souls and God are synonymous with each other. God is a purified form of the Soul when the Soul has achieved omniscience or Siddha-hood.

Jains do not believe in a God who is the creator of the universe or a God who is judgemental of others. These are the traits of a personal God, as described in other religions. Jainism believes in an impersonal God. A God who is defined as any purified soul. So, even Mahavira is not a God who can interfere in our lives. He is a God whom we can idealize and look up to as a role model for our life choices and activities. He taught us the path to eternal happiness. Gods are the ultimate teachers.

Jain Path

In Jainism, the concept of God is characterized as impersonal and nonjudgmental. Despite this, many Jains express their devotion and hope for divine blessings through the singing of praises and the performance of rituals. It's important to note that, in Jainism, the belief that God will grant specific favors is not a central tenet. Instead, the songs and praises are often seen as a means of seeking peace and solace in the midst of life's challenges. When questioned, practitioners understand that the acts of rituals are not intended to compel specific outcomes from God, but rather to cultivate a sense of tranquility and spiritual connection.

The concept of a creator, judgemental, and interventional God is neither scientific nor practical. How can God support the Indian cricket team and not the opponent? Why would God create evil persons and disastrous events? Why would God judge humans and animals? Gods are role models and not controllers. The concept of God as a purified form of the soul is novel and original in philosophical thinking and aligns more with scientific thought.

उपयोगो लक्षणम् ॥ २.८ ॥
upayogo lakṣaṇam ॥ 2.8 ॥
Sentience is the defining characteristic of the soul
-Tattvarth Sutra

THEORY OF KARMA (कर्म)

The Theory of Karma is derived from the Jain philosophy of the *tattva* (तत्त्व) (Truths). In fact, the Karma Theory indoctrinates the old adages: "You sow what you reap", "There are inevitable consequences of one's actions" and "For every action, there is a reaction." The Karma Theory provides a satisfactory, logical, and even scientific explanation of "why bad things happen to good people." "It is not the will of God," as Jains would say, instead "it is one's own Karma that determines one's fate."

The Karma Theory involves a complex foundation of physical and metaphysical entities, mental-physical activity, and metaphysical processes. Jainism, by far, has the most comprehensive doctrine on the Soul, Karmic particles, and the processes of influx, bonding, modification, and fruition of Karma.

The Theory of Karma can be likened to the Law of Gravity in several ways. Both are complex systems of forces that govern interactions, whether between physical objects or human beings. In the case of gravity, the size and mass of objects determine the attractive forces between them, while in Karma, the thoughts (intentions), speech and actions of individuals generate a multitude of cause-and-effect relationships.

The comparison between Karma and gravity underscores the intricate nature of the interactions that shape our world. Despite the lack of current scientific proof for the Theory of Karma, its existence is not invalidated. Over time, as our understanding of the cosmos deepens, certain aspects of these relationships may become more defined and even quantifiable, similar to how the laws of gravity have been formulated and described.

The significance of this comparison lies in highlighting the interconnectedness of actions and their consequences, whether in the physical realm or in the realm of human behaviour and spiritual beliefs. Both Karma and gravity represent fundamental principles that shape the nature of existence and the interplay of forces that define our reality.

Entities for Karma Theory	**Mental-Physical Activity**	**Metaphysical Processes**
Body **Soul** **Karmic Particles**	**Thoughts** **Speech** **Action**	**Influx** of Karma (कर्म का आस्रव) into the Soul **Intentions** of Virtues and Vices (गुण और दोष के भाव) influence the Karmic Particles **Intensity** of Virtues and Vices (गुण और दोष की तीव्रता) influence the binding of Karmic Particles **Bonding** of Karmic Particles (कर्मों का बंधन) to the Soul **Modification** of Karma (कर्म का संशोधन) **Fruition** of Karma (कर्म का फल) to create a situation **Impact** of Catalyst (निमित्त) in situation **Impact** of Effort (पुरुषार्थ) in situation **Choice** of the Soul (आत्मा का चुनाव) in a situation in the form of a Thought, Speech or Action.

Theory of Karma in Diagrammatic Form:

Since the metaphysical is never easy to comprehend with words alone, diagrams can help us better understand the depth and integrities of the Jain Theory of Karma.

Soul with karma

Key Entities are Body, Soul and Karmic Particles

Our soul in present-day life is not experiencing its fullest potential of infinite awareness, knowledge, energy, and bliss. What is holding the soul down from experiencing this full potential and possibilities are karmic particles that attach and detach with every thought, speech, and action we do. In Jainism, these karmic particles are believed to be material objects (*karma vargana* कर्म वर्गणा) that attach to the non-material soul.

Jain Path

Thought Speech and Action lead to influx of karmic particles:

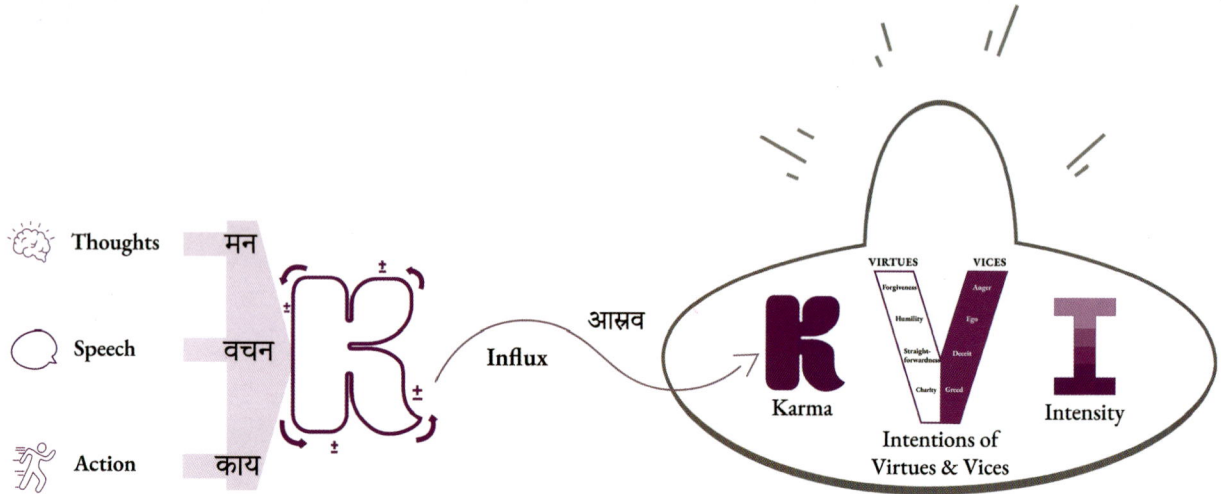

Influx of Karmic Particles

Any activity is in the form of thought (*mana* मन), speech (*vachan* वचन), or action (*kay* काय), and it leads to the influx (*asrava* आस्रव) of Karmic Particles into the soul.

Five reasons for the influx of Karma are 1. Wrong knowledge (*agyan* अज्ञान), 2. Lack of Effort (*pramad* प्रमाद), 3. Lack of Discipline (*avirati* अविरति) 4. Vices (*kshaiya* कषाय) 5. The vibration of soul (*yoga* योग)

A quote from Mahatma Gandhi shows the impact of our thoughts, speech, and actions on our future or destiny.

"Your beliefs become your thoughts,
Your thoughts become your words,
Your words become your actions,
Your actions become your habits,
Your habits become your values,
Your values become your destiny."

Influx of Karma based on the Intentions of Vices and Virtues:

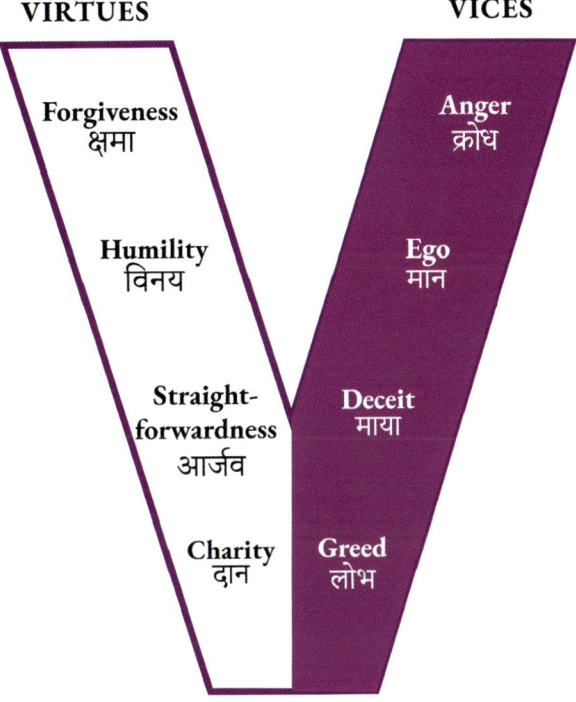

Intentions are Virtues and Vices

Which type of Karma comes into our Soul depends on the Intention, which are our vices or virtues. If the intention is a Vice such as anger, ego, deceit, or greed, then negative karma (*ashubh karma* अशुभ कर्म) inflows and attaches to the soul.

If intentions are Virtues such as forgiveness, humility, straightforwardness, or charity, then positive karma (*shubh karma* शुभ कर्म) inflow and are attached (*samparayika asrava* सम्परायिक आसव). If the action is done without desire for an outcome or with indifference then the Karmic particle flow into the soul and do not attach to the soul (*iryapathic asrava* ईर्यापथिक आसव)

Bonding of the Karma based on Intensity:

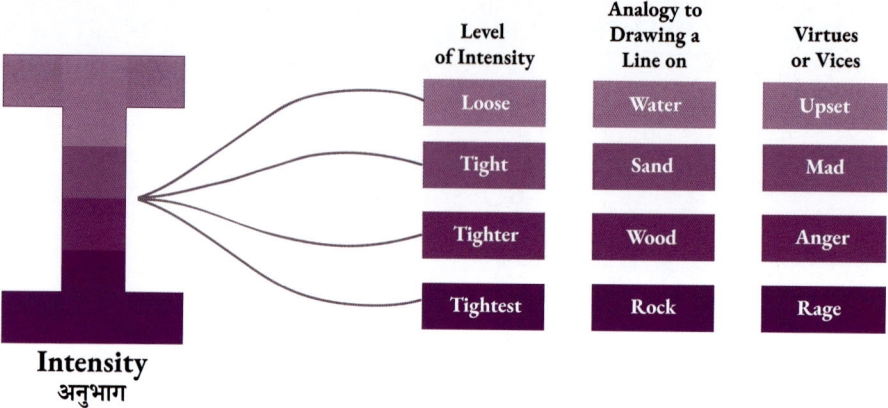

Intensity of Virtues + Vices

Intensity of the vices or virtues determines the strength of the karmic bond between the particle and the soul. Intensity is of four types.

1. Not-Loose
2. Tight
3. Tighter
4. Tightest

An analogy can be made to the drawing of a line in water, sand, wood, and rock. A vice has various intensities of binding, as demonstrated with anger. The binding of karma to the soul is "not tight" when one is upset, "tight" when one is mad, "tighter" when one is angered, and "tightest" when one is enraged.

Likewise, for the virtues the binding is impacted by the strength of intention, such as being tolerant, understanding, forgiving, and compassionate. The karmic particle with intention or vice of virtue with the intensity of the intention determines the karmic bond with the soul. The intentions and intensity change the State of Mind (*leshya* लेश्या). These states of mind are divided into indiscretion (*avivek* अविवेक) and discretion (*vivek* विवेक).

The story of six hungry men and a mango tree where one wants to uproot the tree, another wants to cut its trunk, another wants to break a limb, another wants to shake the branch, another wants just to pluck the fruit, and another wants to pick the fallen fruit from the ground, signifies the various level of state of mind or *leshya* and harm one can do and the level of karmic bondage that occurs with a given action.

The Nature Quantity, Duration and Intensity of Karma:

Jainism describes Karmic particles in great detail with properties that include Nature - *prakriti* (प्रकृति), Quantity -*pradesha* (प्रदेश), Duration -*sthiti* (स्थिति), and Intensity - *anubhag* (अनुभाग). The nature of the bond and the types of karma are reflected by the inherent qualities of the soul and the body.

- The soul related qualities (*ghati* घाति karma) lead to the obstructive karma of awareness, knowledge, energy and bliss (*jnanavarnaiya* ज्ञानावरणीय, *darshanavarnaiya* दर्शनावरणीय, *antaraya* अन्तराय, *mohaniya* मोहनीय,).
- The body-related qualities still coming from the soul (*aghathi* अघाति karma) lead to limitations or changes in physical, age, health, and environment (*vedaniya* वेदनीर, *nama* नार, *gotra* गोत, *ayushya* आरुष) do not affect the soul directly but have a definite and deep impact on the soul through the body.

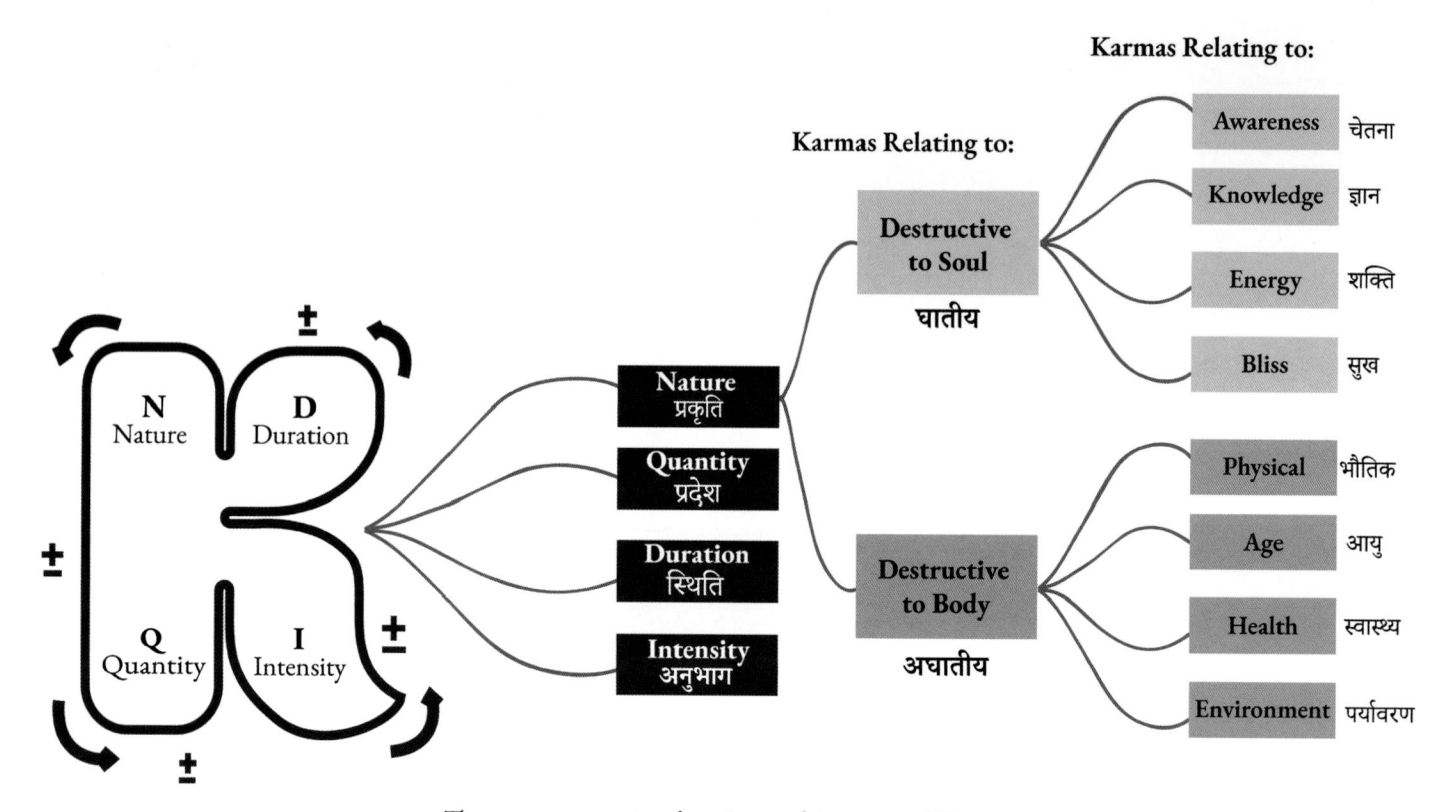

The nature, quantity, duration and intensity of Karma

How to stop the inflow and attachment of Karma -Samvar (संवर):

Jainism brings to the spotlight 5 ways to stop the fresh inflow and attachment of Karma, namely: *samyaktva* (सम्यक्त्व) or right conviction and right knowledge, *vratas* (व्रत) -observance of vows, *apramadu* (अप्रमाद) - awareness or spiritual-alertness *akashaya* (अकषाय) being without vices, and *ayoga* (अयोग)- the peacefulness of mental, verbal and physical activities.

Jain Philosophy

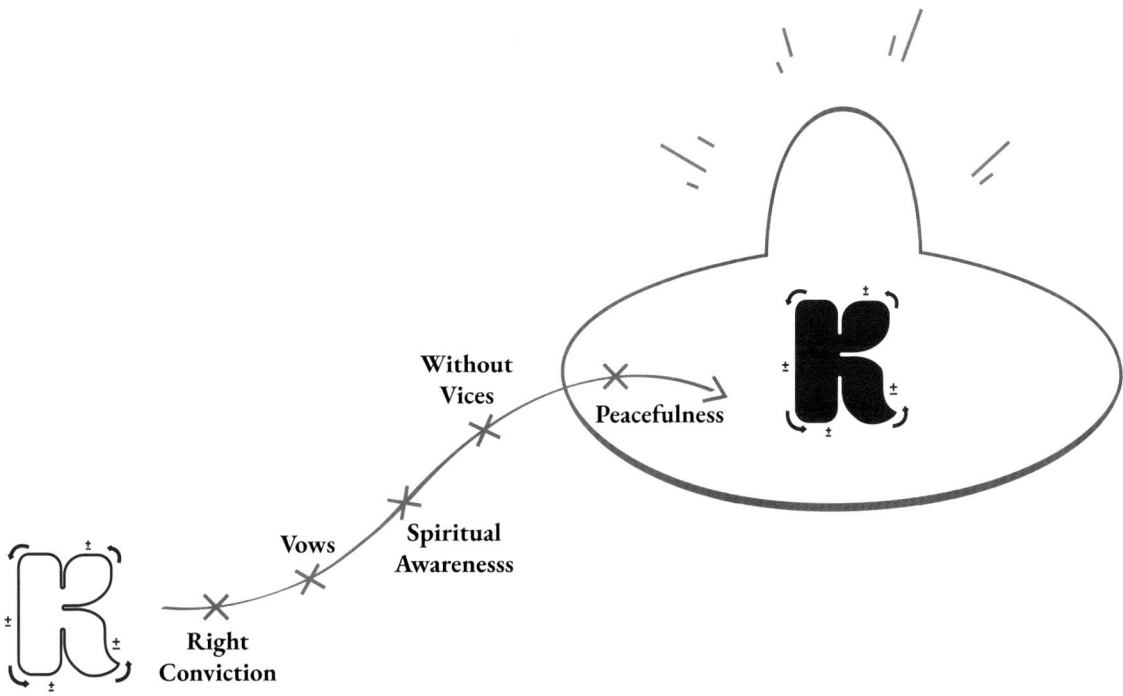

How to stop inflow and attachment of karma - samvar

These are further defined in 57 practical ways to stop the inflow and attachment of karmas:

- They include 5 *samitis* (समिति) or carefulness in our activities like proper walking or speaking.
- The 3 *guptis* (गुप्ति) or restraint in our activities like proper control of our mind, speech, and body.
- The 10 *yati* (यति) dharma or religious virtues which include forgiveness and nonattachment.
- The 12 *bhavanas* (भावना) or *anupreksha* (अनुप्रेक्षा) or reflections that are knowing the impermanence of the world and separateness of the soul.
- The 22 *parishaya vijaya* (परिशय विजय) or victory over 22 hardships such as hunger, thirst, and cold.
- The 5 *charitra* (चारित्र) or conduct such as to remain in equanimity to live without *kashaya* (कषाय).

Binding of Karmic Material to Soul- *Bandha* (बंध)

The binding of Karma to the Soul involves multiple steps that strike a resemblance with that of a mathematical equation:

Bonded Karma = Inflow of Karma (through thought, speech or action) + Intention of Karma (Virtue or Vices) + Intensity of Karma (Loose or Tight)

Once your Karmas are bound to the soul, then they can be modified or they result in fruition.

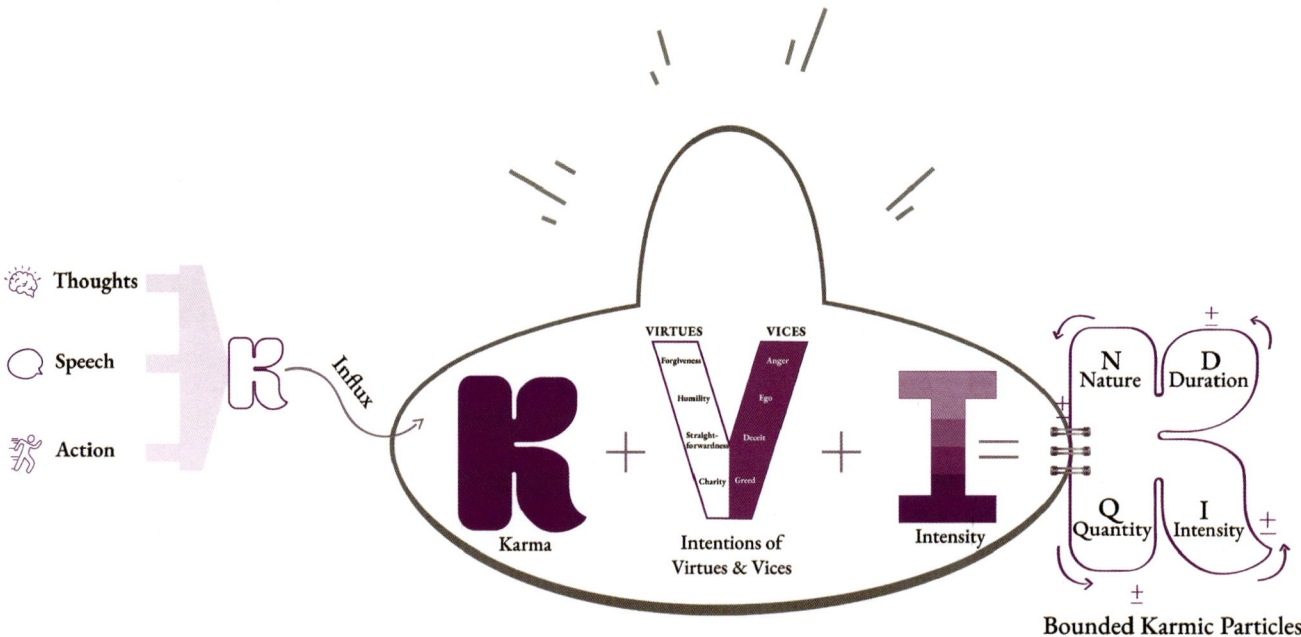

Binding of Karmic Particles

Fruition and Modification of Karma:

Once Karma Particles have bonded to the soul they can undergo modifications of ten types. The natural course is the fruition of karma (*uday* उदय); the fruition results in a particular situation where the soul experiences pleasure or pain. The reaction or activity in terms of thought, speech, and action of the soul in the situation then restarts the cycle of influx of karma. If the soul remains equanimous, it does not add new karma. Other modifications of the karma include dormancy, intensification, dilution, premature operation, interchange suppression, flexibility, and inflexibility.

Impact of Effort (*purshartha* पुरुषार्थ) and a Catalyst called (*nimit* निमित्त) in a given Situation leads to a Free Choice of Thought, Speech and Action:

When karma comes to fruition, it determines a particular Situation, that is based on five factors and explained by an analogy of a mango.

First, it has to be at a particular time (*kaal* काल), A mango has to be ripe, which requires time; the same is true for a given karma.

Second, it must be in its nature for the situation. It is in the nature of the mango tree to bear mangoes and not bear lemons. Likewise, a particular karma that relates to knowledge will relate to an outcome of knowledge.

Third is the effort (*purshartha* पुरुषार्थ) by the soul, The soul can have an impact through its own effort. Only humans have this free choice and the ability to make an effort for a better outcome.

Fourth is the catalyst (*nimit*). Heat is a catalyst that is available for the mango to ripen.

Finally, within the Situation, a Soul has a Free Choice on how to react and do an activity manifested as a Thought, Speech, or Action (TSA). It is this TSA that restarts a new cycle of *karma* (कर्म).

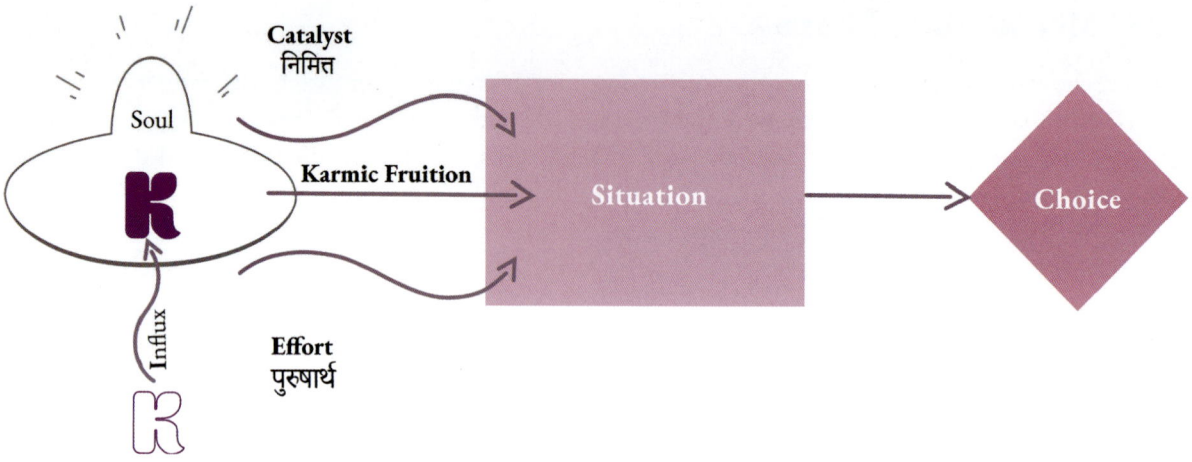

Impact of effort and a catalyst called 'Nimit' in a given situation leads to free choice of thought, speech and action

Entire karmic cycle - from TSA to Influx with Intention and Intensity and Fruition and Free Choice:

Having understood all the entities and processes, it is now possible to comprehend the entire cause-effect of the Karma Cycle.

Any situation is created by several factors, most significant of which are one's own effort (*purushartha* पुरुषार्थ), a catalyst (*nimit* निमित्त) and the fruition of past karma - which we sometimes even called luck. All this creates a Situation in which we are in. In this Situation or an event or circumstance, the soul has to make a Choice which it manifests in the form of a Thought, Speech or Action. An activity of Thought, Speech or Action leads to the influx of Karma particles in the soul, which then binds to the soul based on the intentions expressed by the Vices (anger, ego, deceit, and greed) or Virtues (forgiveness, humility, straight-forwardness, generosity) along with the Intensity of these intentions. Once bonded, the karma can move towards modification or fruition and once there is fruition, it leads to a new Situation or an event.

Jain Philosophy

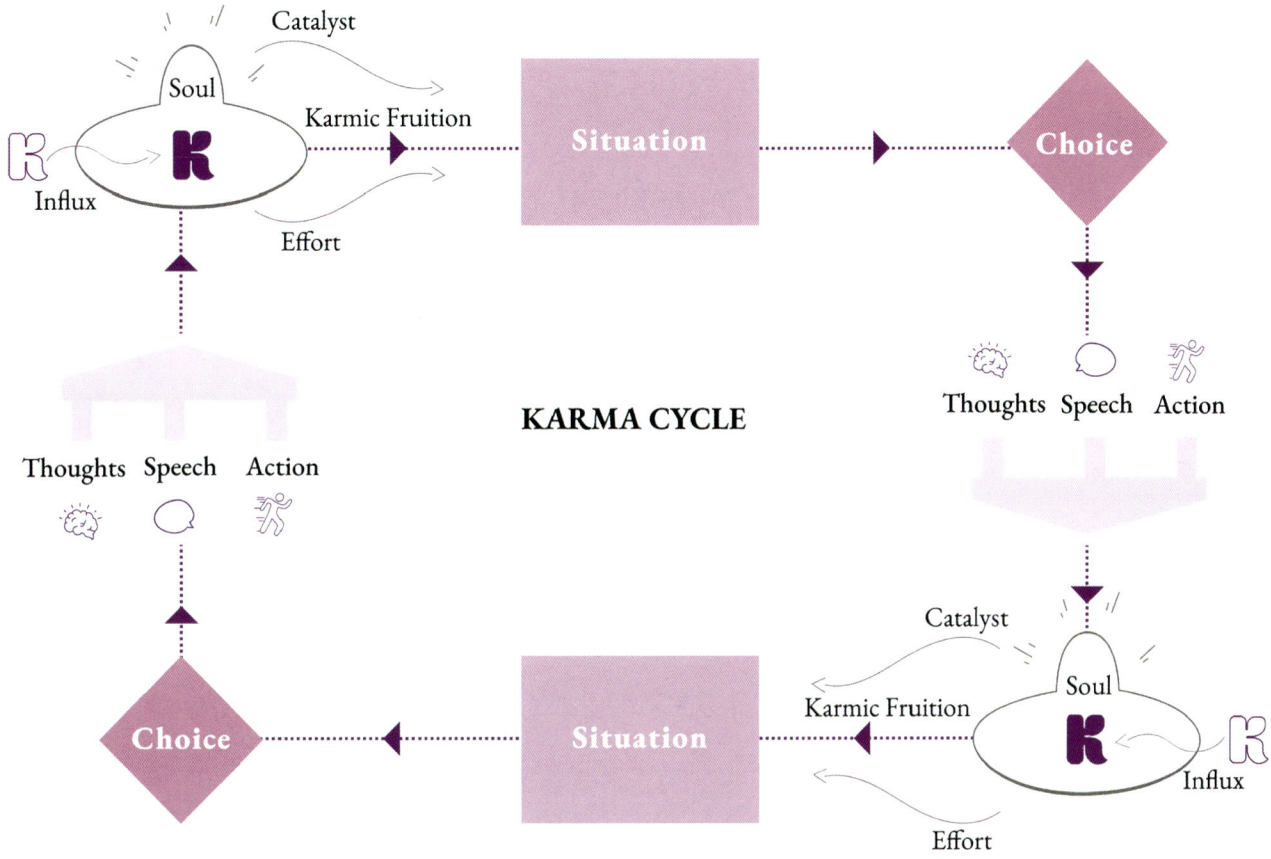

It is essential to take the theory and apply it to our major life events. To see what is determined by our karma, what is dependent on our effort (*purushartha* पुरुषार्थ), and what is a result of a catalyst (*nimit* निमित्त) as an outside agent.

The table illustrates this clearly.

How Karmas and Effort (*purusharth*) Determine Major Life Circumstances: Life Examples

LIFE CIRCUMSTANCES	BIRTH	COLLEGE	CAR ACCIDENT	CAREER	COMPANION	CITY OF RESIDENCE	POSSIBLE DEATH
Your Karma	- Place, family time, gender - Physical features - Mental capacity	Having the mental capacity or secure home to study	The time of being on the road	A friend tells you about job opportunity	Go to same college Parents know each other	Past karma give opportunity to travel abroad	Your genetics and family history
Your Effort (Purushartha)	None	- Your work in high school studying and activities - Study for SAT/ACT	- Safe driver - Do not drink and drive - Drive at speed limit	- Prepare for interview - Do well in school	- You approach others - Respectful dating	Study and work hard	- Smoking - Poor diet - Lack of exercise
Other Forces Catalyst (Nimit)	Mother being close to a hospital if complications or having a healthy lifestyle	Help from parents or teachers	- Drunk driver on road or on road obstruction - Laws passed against drunk drivers	Job opens up when you are looking	A friend introduces you to a companion when you are looking	- Others tell you about it - Job offer comes from city	- Good hospital available at time of illness - Doctor trained in procedure

Example of Karma and car accident

Each and every moment of our existence, we are attracting and shedding karmas. It is these karmas that create pleasure and pain in our lives. Let's look at an event that may happen to you in the future and see how to think about this from a karmic perspective. Suppose, on your way home from school or work tomorrow you get into a car accident. According to Jainism, this is not a random event or a Situation, but rather a confluence of forces which include your past karma, your effort (*purusharth*), and catalyst (*nimit* निमित्त) which determines this event. Once the event happens, the karma is shed and no longer attached to the soul. Your effort in being a safe driver and driving the speed limit may have saved you from a worse accident. The *nimit* (निमित्त) or catalyst like construction on the road or a drunk driver on the other side may have contributed to the accident. After the event is over, your reaction is critical in determining future karmas.

If your reaction to the situation in the form of a thought, speech, and action is of calmness, feeling of forgiveness, and compassion, then positive new karma gets attached; if it is negative anger, animosity, or feeling of revenge, then bad karmas are attached and if it is accepting of the inevitable situation then no new karmas are inflowing or attached.

All the vectors or forces that lead to a Situation are not fully understood by us in our present state of karmic knowledge obstruction. Yet, through better awareness, the karmic consequences are better understood. Also making an effort, such as driving with attentiveness at the speed limit all lead to the prevention of future situations that may lead to an accident.

The karma theory is complex and detailed. Though it may not be easy to accept, there are many good reasons to believe in Karma theory. Here are some reasons to believe in Karma Theory based on JAINA Education Series books.

Why should we believe in the theory of karma?

- Provides a satisfactory explanation for otherwise inexplicable divergences in existence
- It has logic even though it lacks rigorous scientific validation
- Makes each being self-reliant and responsible for their own deeds without reliance on God
- Enforces an ethical behavior and leads to voluntary healthy effort
- Provides high moral conduct by willing common consent
- Not fatalistic, not individualistic, not mechanical and not retributive
- Acceptance of inevitable and inescapable results so as to avoid unnecessary discontentment
- Not about "name shame blame" retribution or punishment rather it is about continuous efforts and improvement for moral regeneration and continuous upliftment of all beings
- Brings peace and prosperity to our society and the world

> स गुप्तिसमितिधर्मानुप्रेक्षापरीषहजयचारित्रैः ॥ ९.२ ॥
> sa guptisamitidharmānuprekṣāparīṣahajayacāritraiḥ ॥ 9.2 ॥
> Inflow is inhibited by guarding, careful movement, morality,
> reflection, conquering hardships, and enlightened conducts
>
> *-Tattvarth Sutra*

THEORY OF MOKSHA (मोक्ष)

The theory of Moksha is of fundamental importance when one is walking on the path of Jainism. Moksha is the destination that is reached through the soul's continuous self-improvement journey. The shedding of karmic bondage is the outcome measure by which a soul can gauge its progress. Jain sages have defined *gunasthanas* (गुणस्थान) or stages of spirituality. The steps for a layperson to move to these stages are called *pratimas* (प्रतिमा).

A Jain must ask, "What is Moksha or *nirvana* (निर्वाण) (used synonymously), and why should it matter to me?" The Jain Way of Life simplifies the steps, yet the destination remains the same. The First step is to do no harm to oneself and others, having no pain and suffering. Second, it is to have the present happiness of daily joys and pleasures of life and family. The third step is to bring equanimity, which is a state of lasting happiness without the daily ups and downs of pleasures and pains. The fourth and last step is to attain moksha, which is to be free from the karmic bondage and the cycle of birth and rebirths, which leads to eternal happiness.

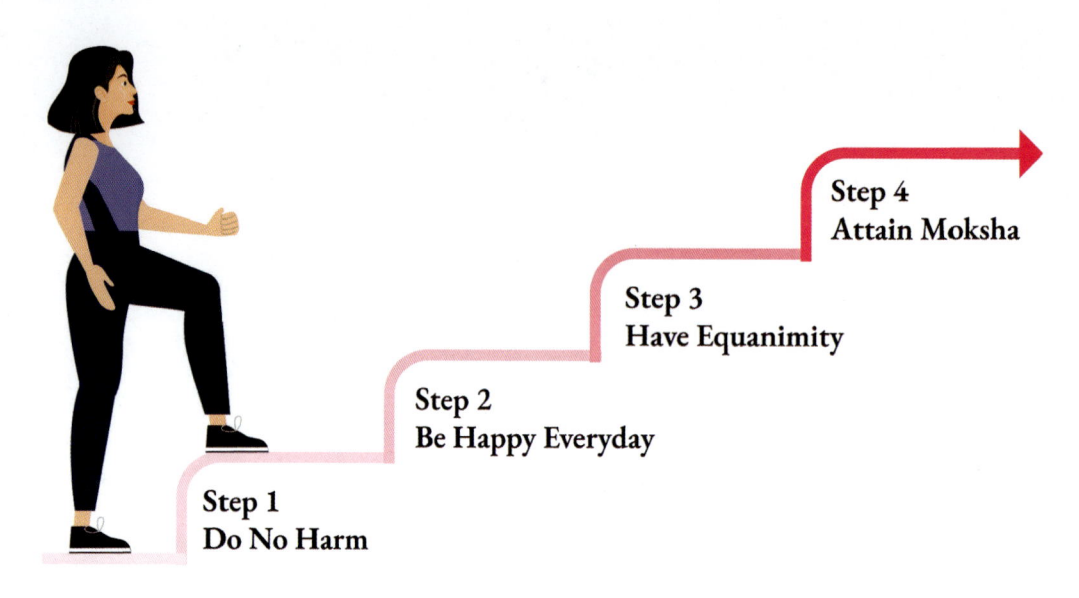

Journey to Happiness Equanimity, and Moksha

Journey to Happiness Equanimity, and Moksha

Step 1: Do no harm to self and others
Step 2: Take joy and pleasure in daily activities — Present Happiness
Step 3: Have Equanimity - diminished pains or pleasure — Lasting Happiness
Step 4: Attain Moksha - no cycles of rebirth — Eternal Happiness

Present Happiness: It is joy or pleasure. The sweet taste of chocolate or the pleasing fragrance of a rose gives us pleasure. This is happiness when our vices: anger, ego, deceit, and greed, are limited. Material comforts or a gift can provide us with present happiness. Inherent in the meaning of present happiness is unhappiness, which occurs when the pleasure from the taste or smell is gone.

Lasting Happiness: It is contentment or equanimity that creates lasting happiness. They are states of low levels of vices or nearly elimination of vices. So even when the condition is unfavorable, one is able to remain calm. It is achieved through powerful tools like self-reflection with the aid of mindfulness and overcoming excessive material wants.

Eternal Happiness: It is the experience of the soul or *atma* (आत्मा). It is the state of bliss or moksha, which is achieved with a journey on the spiritual path. Moksha is a state of purity of the soul with infinite awareness, infinite knowledge, infinite energy, and infinite bliss. The soul is omniscient, all-knowing of all cause-effect relationships happening in the universe. In simple words, when our soul achieves Moksha, we are God. Hence, Jainism takes the principle of equality to the greatest extreme that there is not just equality of race, religion, gender, and all living beings, but also the potential of achieving equality and one with God in the state of moksha.

The path to liberation in our eternal lives and the path to equanimity in our present life is through constantly following the three-fold way of Strong Faith, Enlightened Knowledge, and Spiritual Conduct. From ancient scriptures, the elements of faith, knowledge, and conduct are analogs to modern science's KAP process or Knowledge, Attitude, and Practice, all of which are required for any change to happen.

The first verse of the first chapter of the sacred Jain text *Tattvartha Sutra* (तत्वार्थ सूत्र), written 1800 years ago, says "*samyak-darshana-jnana-charitrani moksamargah*" (सम्यक-दर्शन -ज्ञान -चरित्राणि -मोक्षमार्गः) The strong faith, enlightened knowledge and spiritual conduct is the path to liberation.

Samyak Darshan (Strong Faith सम्यक-दर्शन): *Samyak Darshan* is an unwavering faith in the soul. The belief that the soul exists, that it is independent, and that I am the soul. It is not faith in one's body or mind or even blind faith in Jainism itself.

Samyak Jnän (Enlightened Knowledge सम्यक-ज्ञान): *Samyak* Jnän is knowledge about the Truths. The truths of Taatv are that the soul is different from the body and the theory of karma, knowledge of the operation of Karma, and its relationship to the Soul.

Samyak Charitra (Disciplined Conduct सम्यक चारित्र): *Samyak Charitra* expects one to adhere to Jain principles of Ahimsa, *Anekantavada*, and *Aparigraha* and practices such as vegetarianism, forgiveness and charity.

Summary - Theory of Life, Soul, Karma and Moksha

Philosophy is the foundation of our thinking. It shapes, determines, and impacts deeply and profoundly on how we think about ourselves and the universe around us. There are many competing philosophies that we are surrounded by in today's day and age. Some of these are new, and some are centuries, even thousand years old. Jain philosophy offers us an option that is grounded in both the physical and the metaphysical. The physical relationship relates to the theory of life, the living and nonliving, and knowing the difference. Jain philosophy then delves deeply into the metaphysical with belief in the concepts of Soul, Karma, and Moksha.

Jain Principles - AAA

AHIMSA (NONVIOLENCE)

ANEKANTAVADA (NONABSOLUTISM)

APARIGRAHA (NONPOSSESSIVENESS)

JAIN PRINCIPLES - AAA

The *Tattvartha Sutra* (तत्वार्थ सूत्र) is the single most comprehensive Jain scripture and often called the Bible of the Jains. In the introduction to the translation of *Tattvartha Sutra - That Which is,* Nathmal Tatia, a renowned modern Jain scholar, captures Jain Philosophy in its totality with this opening paragraph.

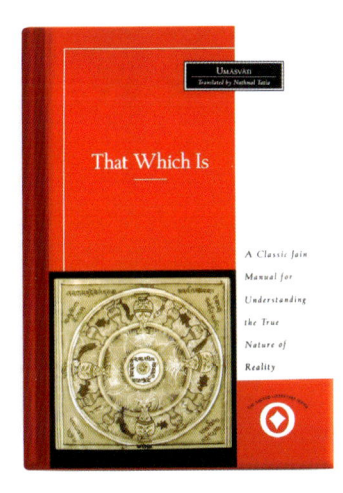

> *"The central themes of the Tattvartha Sutra (तत्वार्थ सूत्र) are Nonviolence (Ahimsa अहिंसा), Nonabsolutism (Anekantavada अनेकांतवाद), and Nonpossessiveness (Aparigraha अपरिग्रह). Nonviolence strengthens the autonomy of life of every being.*
>
> *Nonabsolutism strengthens the autonomy of thought of every individual.*
>
> *Nonpossessiveness strengthens the interdependence of all existence.*
>
> *If you feel that every soul is autonomous, you will never trample on its right to live. If you feel every person is a thinking person, you will not trample on his or her thoughts. If you feel that you own nothing, no one will trample on the planet. In the second century CE, when the Jaina philosopher-monk Umasvati wrote the Tattvartha Sutra these principles were the only way to global peace. Today, this is even more the case. These are the only values that can save humanity from the deadly acts of war, economic exploitation, and environmental destruction."*

The principles of AAA, *Ahimsa* (अहिंसा), *Anekantavada* (अनेकांतवाद), and *Aparigraha* (अपरिग्रह), are derived from Jain Philosophy which can be consolidated into four Jain Theories: Theory of Life, Soul (*atma* आत्मा), Karma (कर्म), and Moksha (मोक्ष). The three Principles of *Ahimsa, Anekantavada,* and *Aparigraha* lead to the core Jain practices such as Vegetarianism/Veganism, Forgiveness, Compassion, Yoga and Exercise, Respect, Open-mindedness, Meditation, Balancing Consumerism, Art of Dying, and Environmentalism.

The AAA *Ahimsa* (अहिंसा), *Anekantavada* (अनेकांतवाद), and *Aparigraha* (अपरिग्रह)) are not random principles rather they have an underlying unifying goal: Equity. Equity is different from equality. Equality is an equal amount for all, equity is provided so all reach to an equal level; hence equity has an element of fairness and justice.

Equality is different from equity

For a moment, imagine a world of equity.

- Imagine Equity for all living beings. Equity of all human beings. Equity of all races, religions, and genders.
- Imagine Equity of all thoughts. Equity and respect of all viewpoints, and tolerance of all whom we agree and disagree with.
- Imagine Equity in our basic needs. Equity in the availability of food, clothing, shelter, and health care for all.

Such is the planet that the Jain sages imagined when they originated the principles of Ahimsa-equity of all living beings, *Anekantavada*-equity of all perspectives, and *Aparigraha*-equity of basic needs. Humankind is evolving towards Equity.

Even at the time of Mahavira, Jainism was ahead of its time in recognizing social equity of the four classes in society: *Brahmin* (learned class ब्राह्मण), *Kshatriya* (warrior class क्षत्रिय), *Vaishya* (business class वैश्य), and *Shudra* (untouchables or working-class शूद्र). No caste system existed or exists even today in Jainism.

Jain Principles - AAA

AHIMSA
Nonviolence

My Soul = Other's Soul

All Life has Right to Live

ANEKANTAVADA
Nonabsolutism

My Perspective = Other's Perspective

All Perspective are Respected

APARIGRAHA
Nonpossessiveness

My Basic Needs = Other's Basic Needs

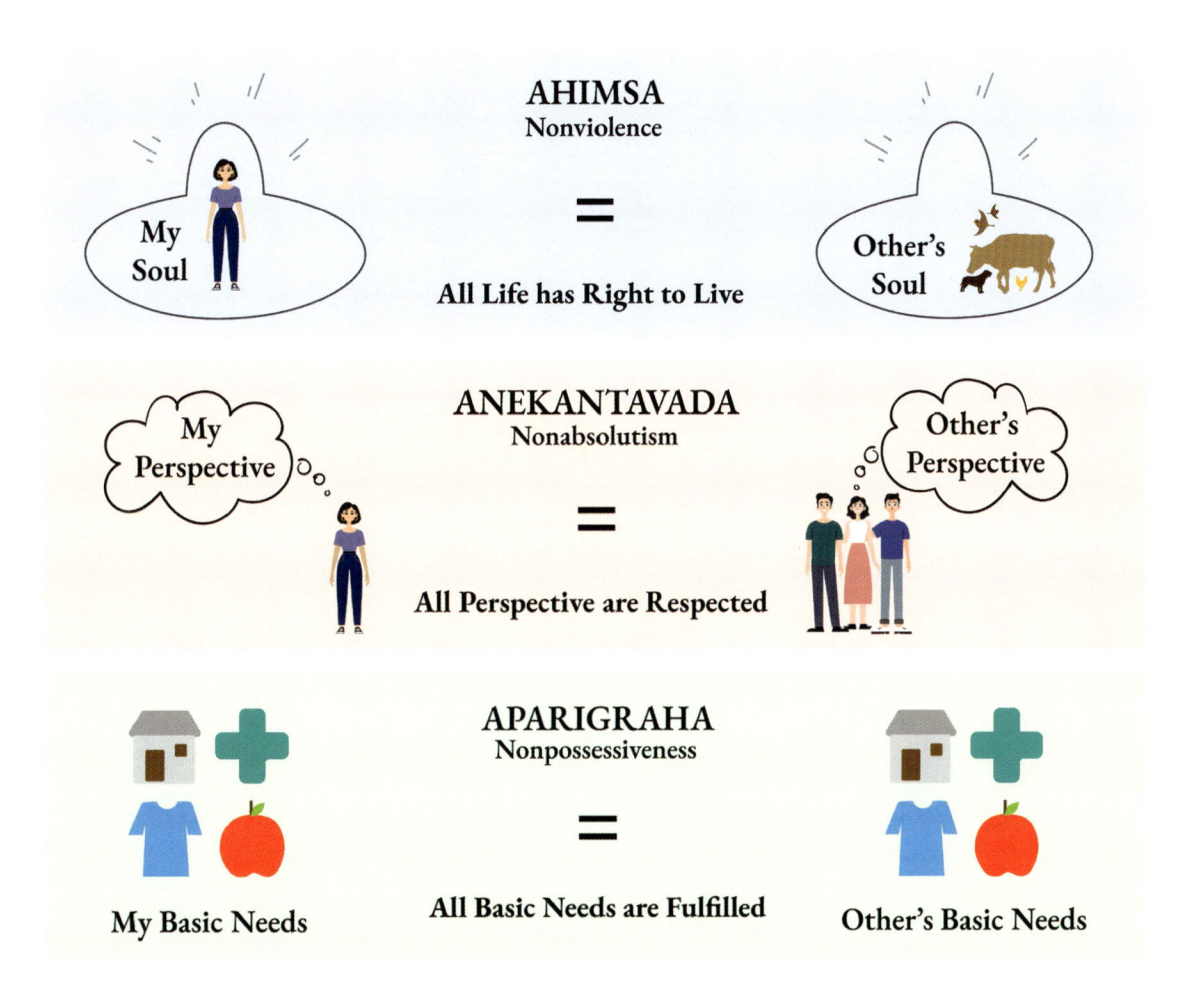

All Basic Needs are Fulfilled

Ahimsa, Anekantavada, and Aparigraha are derived from the fundamental value of Equity of all souls, all perspectives, and everyone's basic needs.

AHIMSA (NONVIOLENCE)

Ahimsa (अहिंसा) *Nonviolence*

Ahimsa to Jains is a religion. It is the ultimate ethic and a way of life, *"Ahimsa parmo dharma"* (अहिंसा परमो धर्म).

Nonviolence is the ultimate religion. It has been this way since the beginning of documented Jain history from the time before Parasnath and Mahavira. Just as Buddhism's central focus is the "Middle way, " Jainism's single focus is Ahimsa.

Often, the other two principles of *Anekantavada* (अनेकांतवाद) and *Aparigraha* (अपरिग्रह) are said to be subsets of Ahimsa. *Anekantavada* is not harming others by respecting others' perspectives, and *Aparigraha* is not hurting others by limiting our own possessions so that the basic needs of others are met.

To better understand the principle of ahimsa in its great depth it is important to understand the genesis and evolution of ahimsa through the lens of eastern and western history. Then, we can see how Ahimsa is embedded in our lives by understanding the "what, who, how, and why" of Ahimsa. What is Ahimsa? Toward who to be Ahimsic? How to practice Ahimsa? Why practice Ahimsa?

Genesis and Evolution of Ahimsa

In times past, when one came into conflict over land, money, mate, or religion, the usual way to resolve the conflict was to fight, duel, deceive, or kill the opponent and let the mightiest win. Such has been the general thought and way of solving problems. Since a large part of the world has taken this path; unfortunately, war, holocausts, genocides, torture, and rape are and have been the modus operandi and the main method to resolve conflicts and disagreements.

Some 5,000 years ago, thinkers in the East pursued the solution to conflicts in a completely unique way. Instead of violence (often called the animal instinct by Gandhi), the sages pursued a nonviolent approach. "Could all of man's conflicts with one another, with other living beings, with nature (global warming), and even with oneself (such as addiction and stress) be resolved nonviolently as the central universal ethic? Could this be the defining difference between humans and animals?" These evolutionary thinkers were from the Sramanic tradition in the East. The Sramans were distinct from the Brahmins, who practiced the Vedic traditions of rituals and sacrifices, in contrast to the Sramans, who practiced austerities, and nonviolence in their thought, speech, and action.

Jain Principles - AAA

How has nonviolence evolved over the millennia? Who were its proponents in the East and the West who fundamentally changed the course of the understanding of the practice of nonviolence?

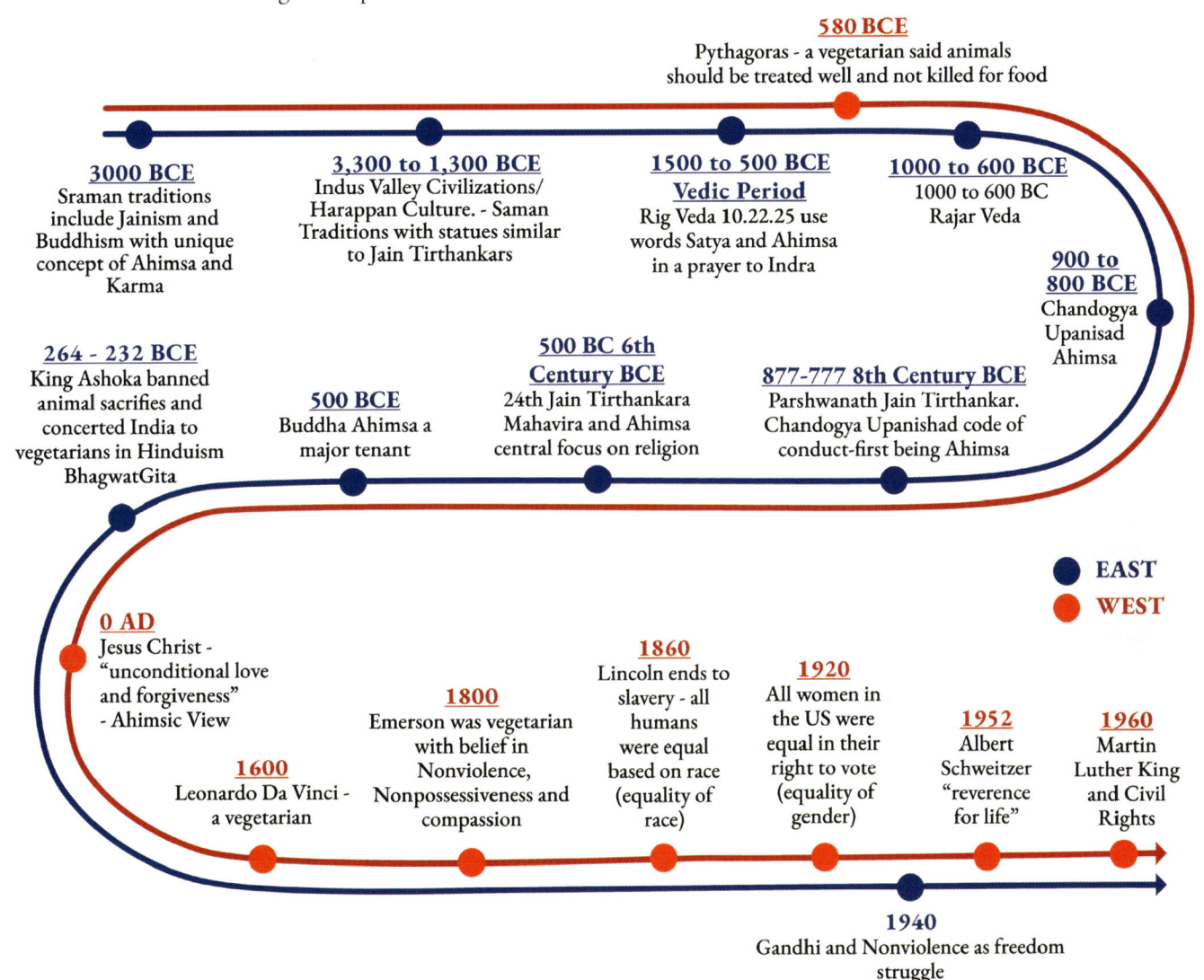

580 BCE
Pythagoras - a vegetarian said animals should be treated well and not killed for food

3000 BCE
Sraman traditions include Jainism and Buddhism with unique concept of Ahimsa and Karma

3,300 to 1,300 BCE
Indus Valley Civilizations/ Harappan Culture. - Saman Traditions with statues similar to Jain Tirthankars

1500 to 500 BCE
Vedic Period
Rig Veda 10.22.25 use words Satya and Ahimsa in a prayer to Indra

1000 to 600 BCE
1000 to 600 BC
Rajar Veda

900 to 800 BCE
Chandogya Upanisad Ahimsa

264 - 232 BCE
King Ashoka banned animal sacrifices and concerted India to vegetarians in Hinduism BhagwatGita

500 BCE
Buddha Ahimsa a major tenant

500 BC 6th Century BCE
24th Jain Tirthankara Mahavira and Ahimsa central focus on religion

877-777 8th Century BCE
Parshwanath Jain Tirthankar. Chandogya Upanishad code of conduct-first being Ahimsa

● EAST
● WEST

0 AD
Jesus Christ - "unconditional love and forgiveness" - Ahimsic View

1600
Leonardo Da Vinci - a vegetarian

1800
Emerson was vegetarian with belief in Nonviolence, Nonpossessiveness and compassion

1860
Lincoln ends to slavery - all humans were equal based on race (equality of race)

1920
All women in the US were equal in their right to vote (equality of gender)

1952
Albert Schweitzer "reverence for life"

1960
Martin Luther King and Civil Rights

1940
Gandhi and Nonviolence as freedom struggle

39

Estimated Long Term Trend In American Homicide Rate

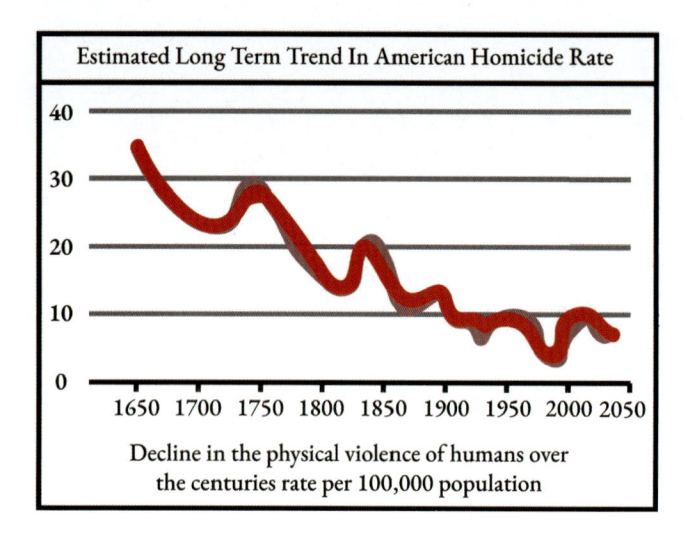

Decline in the physical violence of humans over the centuries rate per 100,000 population

History tells us that Nonviolence is an evolved human behavior while violence is a primitive behavior.

With mass shootings, riots, the ongoing wars, and terrorism, we may feel there is more violence today. Yet, this is because we see our world today from the lens of the 24-7 media, which can hyperbolize an event to billions of people in a matter of seconds. While ages ago, there were few or no laws to protect against murder, rape, or physical abuse and they would go unreported and unquestioned.

Violence on the battlefield also killed millions. Studies show that the homicide rate has declined over the past 400 years. So there is not more violence in the world, but more awareness of violence.

Ironically, as violence towards humans has declined, the violence towards animals has increased. This is due to industrialization, mass production, processing, and packaging of meat in slaughterhouses, and the presentation of meat in a sanitized way in grocery stores. The awareness of such violence against animals has declined. If one were to see the anguish, pain, and torture of slaughter, then many would reconsider the ethics of eating meat and follow a more nonviolent diet.

Meat consumption increased in Asia and the World

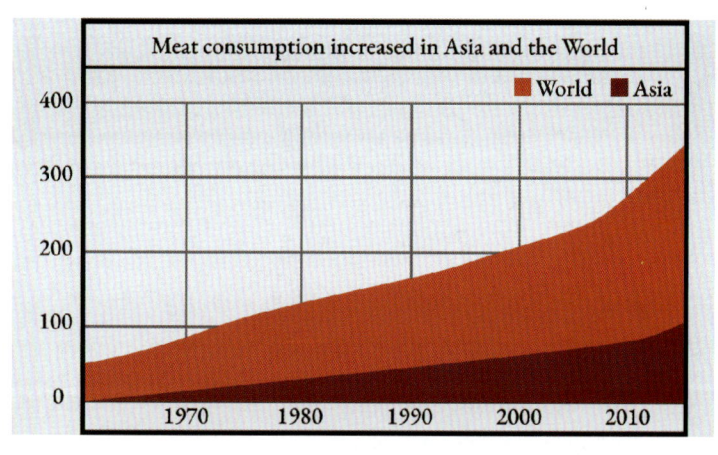

Rise in violence towards animals (meat production) over the past half-century mostly in Asia.

As per the diagrammatic representation shown above, meat production has gone up threefold since the 1970s, mostly in developing countries, to 300 trillion pounds. This reflects the increased number of animals who are being slaughtered.

What is Ahimsa? Know the Tree of Ahimsa

The antidote to violence is nonviolence or Ahimsa. So, what is Ahimsa? While the answer can be profoundly philosophical or simply practical, the many forms of Ahimsa can be revealed in the form of a tree. Practicing the principle of Ahimsa leads to vegetarianism, forgiveness, compassion, and much more.

Ahimsa is like a tree's trunk. From here, there are two major branches: first, to do no harm, and second, to help others. Each of these two paths has three sub-branches relating to how we practice nonviolence by three mediums: our thoughts, our speech, and our actions. And then, each of these mediums is further divided into: doing the activity, getting someone to do the activity, and appreciating when others have done the activity. The branch of ahimsa which is helping others relates to the 4 *bhavanas*: neutrality (*madhyastha* मध्यस्थ), *friendship* (*maitri* मैत्री), *appreciation* (*pramod* प्रमोद), *compassion* (*karuna* करुणा).

An iceberg reflects the method of how violence is done. What is evident on the surface is the action, yet underneath is an attempt and deeper further is intention for violence.

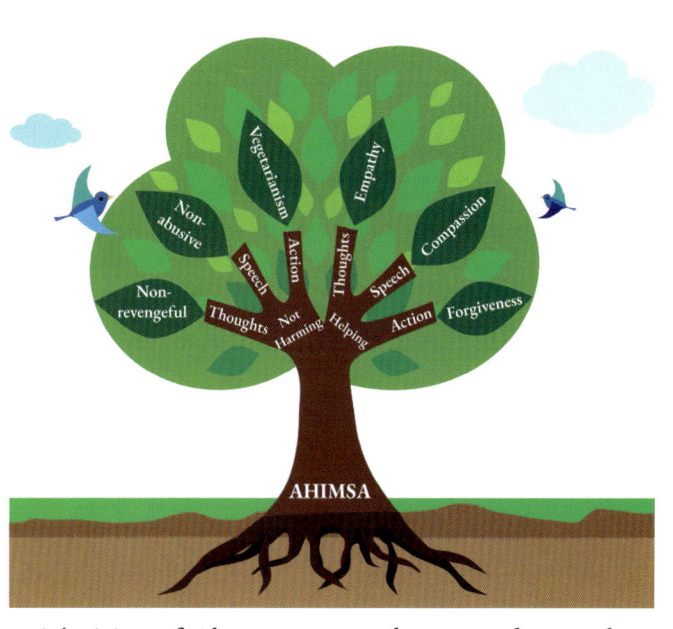

The Tree of Ahimsa is rooted in Equality with branches of different mediums of thought, speech and action and bearing fruits of vegetarianism, forgiveness, and compassion

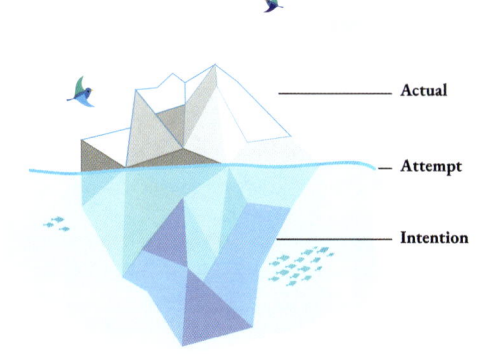

An iceberg reflects the method how violence is done

When we put *Ahimsa* in full display, the *Ahimsa* tree bears fruit in the form of practices that include not hurting, not bullying, vegetarianism, forgiveness, compassion and more.

The tree of *Ahimsa* is rooted in a simple concept of Equality of all living beings. If we believe in equality as the seed, then *Ahimsa* is the tree that is achieved through not harming and helping in the form of our thoughts, speech, and action through our own activity, encouragement of others' activity, or praising of others' activity.

Jain Path

Of the three mediums of how violence or nonviolence is done, Thoughts or Intentions are the most critical. In fact, they are the precursor to violence in our speech and actions. Just think about the difference between a deep cut from a knife of a surgeon or a terrorist. According to Jainism, Intentions or thoughts are the most damaging or beneficial to our soul and incur the most karma.

In Jainism, the method by which one does violence matters. Think of an iceberg; violence begins with Intention (*bhava hinsa* भाव हिंसा). For instance, if 100 people have an intention, maybe 50 will attempt it. And then only 10 may actually do it (*Dravya Himsa* द्रव्य हिंसा). When we see violence, we need to know the Intentions underneath it.

Minimizing Violence

While not committing any violence is the ideal goal, the Jain sages were practical, and they realized that to survive, one has to commit some level of violence. So they triaged the level of violence based on the level of life force in different levels (*indriya* इन्द्रिय) various living beings have. The life forces are a life span, physical forms, respiratory, touch (sensation स्पर्श), taste (रस), smell (घ्राण), sight (दर्शना), hearing (कर्ण), speech (भाषा), and mind (मन). The greater the number of life forces for a living being, the greater the karmic load of violence is committed.

Each living being has a different level of life force. Hence the karmas accumulated from violence towards a plant is less than that when violence is towards a human.

A Jain parable of six men and a mango tree allows us to see the varying levels of violence.

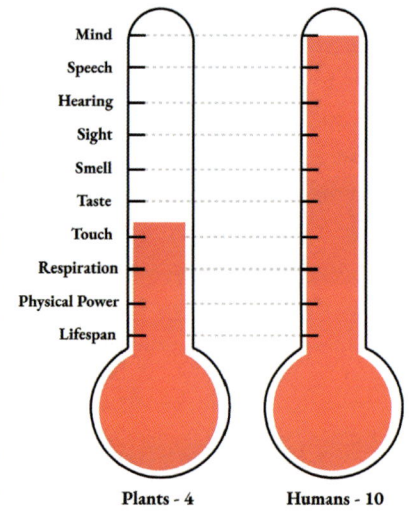

Six hungry men are in a forest when, at a distance, they see a mango tree burgeoning with ripe mangoes on its branches and some on the ground. The first man pulls out his axe and says, "I will chop down the tree and get all the mangoes."

The parable of the six men and the mango tree shows the level of violence, even at the intention level

Varying life forces in various living beings

The second man says, "I will climb up the tree and hack this large branch and get the mangoes."
The third man says, "I will break this small branch and get the mangoes."
The fourth man says, "I will shake the branch and make the mangoes drop."
The fifth man says, "I will just pluck the mangoes that I need."
The sixth man says, "I will pick up the fresh mangoes that are lying on the ground."

The story displays the choice we make each day of how much violence is necessary: a vegetarian diet or a non-vegetarian diet, getting enraged or just being upset, having pity, or being compassionate. Each level of violence and nonviolence determines the karmic burden that our soul incurs. The parable shows the varying state of mind and the varying levels of violence.

The violence of necessity not only exists in our daily lives, but it also exists in our occupations and also in self-protection. For the layperson, all these forms of violence are permitted according to the Jain sages, yet monks renounce these forms of violence.

The violence of necessity occurs in three areas: daily activity, occupation, and self-defense

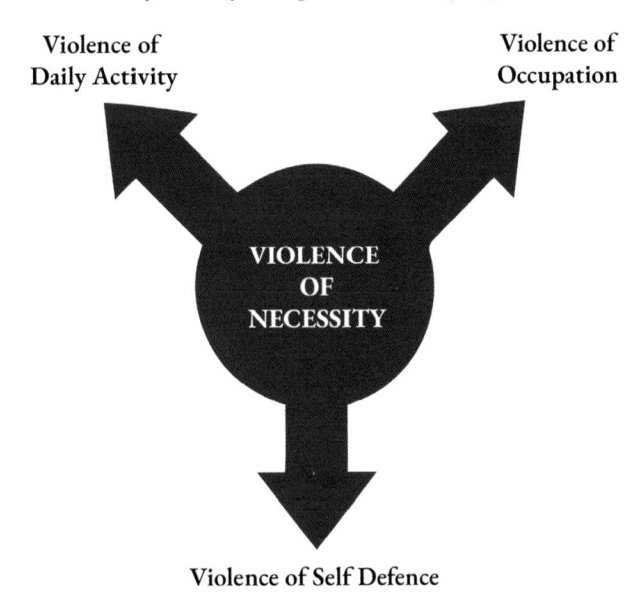

Violence of Daily Activity

Violence of Occupation

VIOLENCE OF NECESSITY

Violence of Self Defence

Ahimsa towards Who? CIRCLE OF AHIMSA

No Smoking, Alchohol and Drugs

SELF

Low Stress

Eating Well

Exercise

Yoga and Meditation

Nonviolence begins with nonviolence towards self

Jainism is clear on our need to be nonviolent. Hence, the question arises: who should we be nonviolent towards? Imagine layers of concentric circles. Now imagine each ring of the circle is a different entity that we need to be nonviolent towards: self, others, animals, environment. Such categorization helps us better understand the depth of nonviolence in Jainism.

Nonviolence towards the Self: Often, we think about violence being committed towards people, animals, or the environment, but we are unaware of the violence towards the self. So how do we commit such self-violence?

Physical self-violence is in the form of self-abuse with smoking, excessive drinking, and illicit drug use. These practices physically harm the body, leading to cancer, heart disease, liver failure, and overdose death, and are unambiguously forbidden in Jainism. Mental self-violence is in the form of overeating, not sleeping, and excessive stress. The solution Jain scriptures suggest for mental self-violence is healthy eating, restful sleep, yoga, and meditation. At a deeper level, there is psychological self-violence that occurs through self-criticism and excessive negative thoughts. For this, Jain Reflections (*bhavanas* भावना) provide solutions to us. Hence, Nonviolence towards the self is avoiding smoking, excessive drinking, illicit drug use, healthy eating, psychological self-observance, and not having negative thoughts. These recommendations are no different than what our primary care doctor provides. Jain scriptures describe these practices as part of the *yati dharma* (यति धर्म) or religious virtues and are derived from the practices of austerities (*tap* तप), renunciation (*tyag* त्याग), nonattachment (*akinchanya* आकिंचन्य).

Nonviolence towards Family and Friends: The next layer in the circle of nonviolence is nonviolence toward our family, friends, and work colleagues. Violence is not just physical, such as domestic abuse, hitting, or bullying, but mental, such as anger, arguing, deception, jealousy, greed, ego, and even withholding information. Material violence toward family is stealing or having greed in family disputes for wealth, land, property, or any other material possessions. Often, most people do not recognize arguing or deceiving as forms of violence. Instead, these actions are promoted as methods of self-advancement and self-promotion in a competitive world.

Jain sages were clear in avoidance of these subtle forms of mental violence and put them clearly as major (vices Kashay कषाय) or the four most severe ones: anger, ego, deceit, and greed. Most often, we commit mental violence with our friends, family members, and work colleagues and are not aware of the damage it does to our relationships, along with the pain and suffering it causes the other person. Most often, each violent thought, speech, or action ignites a cycle of violence with reaction, retaliation, and repetition. This need not be the case in the cycle of violence. Material violence may be taking an unfair share of property or money from a sibling or not providing sufficient help to family or friends when one has the money, time, and contacts to do so. Nonviolence towards others is part of the yati dharmas: forgiveness (*kshama* क्षमा), humility (*mardava* मार्दव), straightforwardness (*arjava* आर्जव), contentment (*shaucha* शौच), truthfulness (*satya* सत्य), self-restraint (*sanyam* संयम).

Jain Path

The most essential nonviolent action we can do towards others is compassion. Jain sages describe four positive, compassionate reflections (*bhavanas* भावना). They are friendship (*maitri* मैत्री), appreciation (*pramod* प्रमोद), compassion and helping (*karuna* करुणा), equanimity (*madhyastha* मध्यस्त). Jainism is a religion of compassion, and compassion is Ahimsa or nonviolence in all forms.

Nonviolence towards Enemies: Gandhi said it is easy to be nonviolent towards or to forgive your family and friends; the real test of forgiveness is when you have to forgive your enemies. In the course of life, we come across people, groups, institutions, and political parties that we, for good or not-so-good reasons, develop a high level of animosity. We define them as our enemies in no uncertain terms, even after considering their views with an open mind. How should we behave with them according to Jainism? While the principle of *Anekantavada* (अनेकांतवाद), which is discussed later helps in this process of self-reflection and awareness, forgiveness is the first step.

An often-asked question is how to deal with people like Hitler. The answer is complicated. First, we need to separate the person from the actions. We must criticize the killings and slaughter as heinous acts of violence separating them from the person. As for the perpetrators of these actions, we need to recognize that they are misguided and live in ignorance, disrespect, and disregard for other living beings. Every attempt must be made for understanding and reconciliation, and when this fails, then violence for self-defense is permitted. The concept of war with our enemies is only permitted in self-defense. There is absolutely no place for a holy war or martyrdom through violence in Jainism.

Jain Principles - AAA

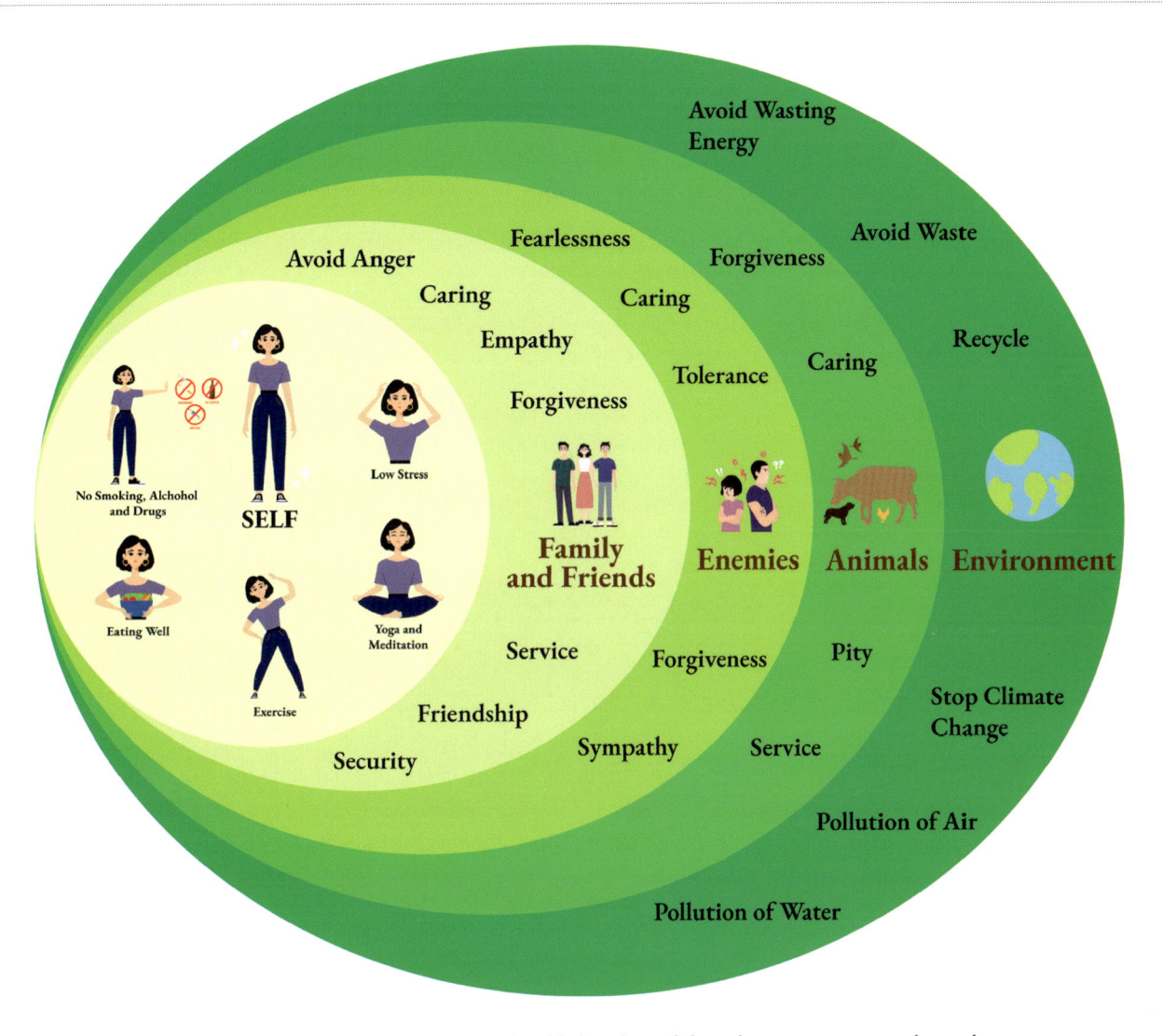

The Circle of Nonviolence: nonviolence towards self, family and friends, enemies, animals, and environment.

47

Nonviolence to Animals:

There is no religion or group of people who adhere to the practice of vegetarianism more strictly than the Jains. Evolution theory discriminates humans from animals only with the presence of an advanced brain, yet even that is questionable. Chimpanzees are able to use tools, and dogs are able to follow 20-30-word commands, which is similar to that of a 2-year-old child.

Animals also have feelings. When we see a mother cow cry with tears when separated from her calf, she certainly feels pain and languishes like a fish flopping out of water when caught in a fishing net.

Jains extend nonviolence to all living beings, to all life and insist on finding ways to minimize violence in daily life. So in food, a vegetarian diet, and now with the suffering industrialization of milk production, a vegan diet is the most nonviolent. Not using silk and avoiding leather products are other ways to prevent harm to animals.

Nonviolence to the Environment:

Mahavira is often called the first environmentalist. In the scriptures, Acharanga Sutra, Mahavira described nature as a living being and that there must be "no waste, no overuse, no abuse, no polluting."

The need to heed this principle is now better than at any other time, with climate changing, glaciers melting, storms raging, and occurrences of extremes in temperature

It is essential to recognize the cycle of violence and nonviolence in our daily lives. Violence begets violence, and nonviolence begets nonviolence. If the person ahead of you holds a door open for you, you are more likely to keep the door open for the person behind you. We reciprocate. If someone cuts you off in traffic, then you are more reckless in your driving and don't bother when you cut off another person. Such actions create cycles of violence and nonviolence in our lives, in our society, and even among nations. So, through self-awareness and reflection, we can break the cycle of violence by a nonviolent act and make sure not to break the cycle of nonviolence through a violent act.

Transformation:

The Jain sages guide us towards a path of happiness. Happiness is joy, pleasure, equanimity, and moksha. To achieve Happiness, a fundamental transformation is required in our thoughts, speech, and actions. How can this transformation happen? Following is stepwise guidance.

Anger can transform into Forgiveness by self-awareness and self-reflection. It also requires a root cause analysis. We need to uncover the reasons someone may have hurt us with empathy. We need to see the situation from the other person's perspective and accept their perspective. We need to accept the fact that harm was done to us and work to move forward by saying sorry. We need to make a conscious effort to work each and every day, not to hold grudges and to reconcile. We need to wish compassion and goodwill towards others.

Hatred can transform into Understanding. It begins with self-awareness and self-reflection. We need to separate the person from their actions and criticize the action, not the person. With empathy, we need to educate ourselves about the person or situation we feel hatred towards. We need to overcome our own insecurities, which often lead to hatred towards others. To reach an understanding, we need to practice non-judgment and see the situations from other's views.

Deceit can transform into straight-forwardness. Begin with self-awareness and self-reflection. We need to cultivate self-acceptance and self-confidence. We need to recognize our own lies and seek support. We must be willing to change and create new habits to achieve straight-forwardness.

Cursing can transform into Complimenting. We may rarely curse someone to their face but may curse them in private, maybe a colleague from work or someone whom we had an argument with. We can change the curse to a compliment by first recognizing why we are cursing. Some action by another person may have provoked us. We need to recognize that when we react in such a manner, we are allowing another person to control us and cause violence within us. We need to recognize other people's faults or actions, but we also need to recognize that they may have done something which is praiseworthy. Think of a compliment and verbalize it, even in private.

Discrimination can transform into equity. We need to recognize that the path to discrimination is through stereotyping, bias, and prejudice. We need to notice how a system of discrimination is putting down a group of people. We can apply the principle of nonviolence and equity towards all. If we begin by seeing the other person as our equal, then we can see them as a person who also has basic needs, feelings, and aspirations similar to ours. Rather than discriminating, we can practice equity towards all individuals.

Jain Path

Transformation is not easy. It is a fundamental change in the way we do things. It is a stepwise approach towards nonviolence. Here are some flow diagram approaches to change. Transformation nearly always begins with awareness and reflection. Then, we need to have knowledge of the action and the implications of the violence. In any situation, we need to have the attitude and desire to change. Then, the most challenging part of the transformation is making a change in our behavior. Over time, we can make the new behavior a habit. The fundamental elements of any transformation are awareness, knowledge, attitude change, and behavior change.

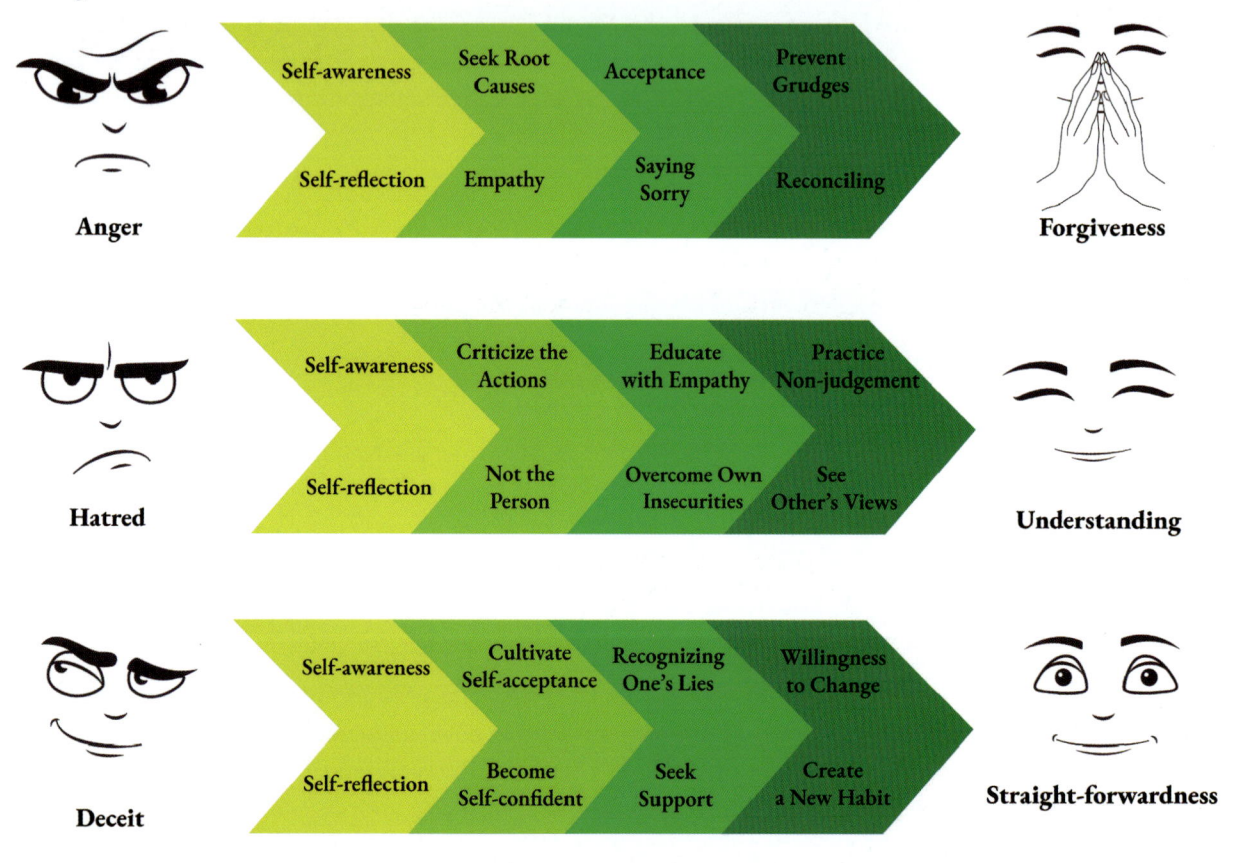

Anger → Self-awareness / Self-reflection → Seek Root Causes / Empathy → Acceptance / Saying Sorry → Prevent Grudges / Reconciling → **Forgiveness**

Hatred → Self-awareness / Self-reflection → Criticize the Actions / Not the Person → Educate with Empathy / Overcome Own Insecurities → Practice Non-judgement / See Other's Views → **Understanding**

Deceit → Self-awareness / Self-reflection → Cultivate Self-acceptance / Become Self-confident → Recognizing One's Lies / Seek Support → Willingness to Change / Create a New Habit → **Straight-forwardness**

How we can transform ourselves.

One fundamental question often asked is: Is the intrinsic nature of humans towards violence or nonviolence? While no definitive answer is available, let's consider this. A baby cries when it is in distress and in pain. It is a signal of stress or violence he or she is experiencing. However, a baby smiles and laughs when he or she is without stress, pain, or fear, which is a sign of nonviolent experience. Neither reaction has to be taught to the baby. Hence both experience of violence and experience of nonviolence are within our nature. As humans, what we need to do is make sincere, constant, and consistent efforts to cultivate nonviolence. Jainism says the intrinsic nature of the soul is nonviolence, but karmic particles can influence us toward violent behavior. Jain philosophy delineates how to lead a life of *ahimsa* (अहिंसा), which is nonviolence towards all human beings as well as towards all living beings and towards the planet.

परस्परोपग्रहो जीवानाम् ॥ ५.२१ ॥

parasparopagraho jīvānām ‖ 5.21 ‖

Souls render service to one another.

-*Tattvarth Sutra*

ANEKANTAVADA (NONABSOLUTISM)

Anekantavada (अनेकांतवाद) Nonabsolutism

Respecting, seeking, and accepting of multiple viewpoints is Anekantavada.

The ancient Jain Sages elevated *Anekantavada* as a fundamental principle necessary for the practitioners of the Jain path. The Jain Sages recognized that:

- Human happiness (as manifested by joy, pleasure, equanimity, and the path to moksha) is hindered by human conflict.
- The root of human conflict is varying perspectives among humans about Reality (Truth).
- Reality (Truth) is complex, and though we can experience this Reality (Truth), we cannot adequately express it due to the limitations of language.

Hence, a fundamental principle was necessary from which we could derive key practices that would help reduce human conflict such as a war among nations and arguments between couples. So originated the principle of *Anekantavada*, which is being non-absolutist, respecting others' views, and having multiple viewpoints.

Evolution of *Anekantavada*

To analyze and achieve a deeper understanding of Jainism, it is important to know how the philosophy of *Anekantavada* originated. Mahavira never used the word *Anekantavada*. However, he sowed the roots of multiplicity of views in his response to the question from his disciples Indrabhuti Gautam and Jayanti from the Jain scripture known as Bhagavati Sutra. Here is an excerpt from their divine conversation:

Gautam: Is the soul permanent or impermanent?

Mahavira: The soul is permanent as well as impermanent.

Jayanti: Of the states of lethargy and awakening, which is desirable or better?

Mahavira: For some souls, the state of lethargy is better for others the state of awakening.

At a superficial level, Mahavira's responses sound "wishy-washy" or indecisive. However, at the philosophical level, they are extremely profound. To Gautam, Mahavira elaborates on this answer.

It (the soul) is permanent with respect to substance (dravya-) which is eternal. It is impermanent with respect to its modes (paryaya) or forms which originate and vanish.

To Jayanti, Mahavira responds.

Lethargy is better for those who are constantly engaged in sinful activities, and awakening or consciousness for those who are engaged in meritorious deeds.

Some centuries after Mahavira, Acharya Siddhansen Divakar coined the term *Anekantavada* and Acharya Umaswami codified it in the 2nd century CE in the *Tattvartha Sutra*. Nearly two millennia later, Mahatma Gandhi said, "I have therefore no objection to calling it (the world) real and unreal, and thus being called an *anekantavadi*."

Jain Path

500 BCE
Mahavira's response to disciples showing multiple perspective

Acharya Kundkund believed in "Anekantavada"

Acharya Siddhasen Divaker coins the word "Anekantavada"

2nd Century CE
Acharya Umaswami in Tattvartha Sutra codifies Anekantavada comprehensively

Syadavada and Nayavada introduce to address Hindu and Buddhist arguments

9th and 13th Century CE
Century reference to Jain parable of Six Blind Men and an Elephant by Vidyanandi and Acharya Mallisena

1926
Mahatma Gandhi in Young India describes himself as Anekantvadi

2000 Modern Day
Religious tolerance, avoiding bias, prejudice and discrimination

1776
Declaration of Independence "that all men are created equal"

● EAST
● WEST

Evolution of Anekantavada

54

Elements of *Anekantavada*:

As the need to resolve human conflict became crucial with each rising day, *Anekantavada* evolved over the centuries. To better understand the depths of *Anekantavada*, let's use diagrams and begin by defining some core entities.

Entities for Anekantavada	Definition
I	Each person has a Perspective and it is distinct from others.
Others	How one sees is different from how others see. Perspective is not reality or the truth, it is how we perceive the outside world.
Perspectives — Ordinary	Ordinary view is when we are unaware and may be open to dialogue. When we see things without awareness or opinion.
Anekantvadi (multi-view)	Anekantvadi view is when we actively are aware of multiple views of a given object, idea or situation.
Absolutist	Absolutist view is when we see things in a particular view and refuse to respect or learn about any other view except our own.
Truth or Reality	Truth or Reality is an object, idea or situation, which is being viewed. While different perspectives exist of this reality. One ultimate truth does exist, however often we are not able to capture it in totality as humans. Also, while we can all experience the truth we cannot express or verbalize as humans.

To understand Anekantavada it is important to know the core elements: the self, others, ordinary perspective, Anekantavadi (follower of multi-views अनेकांतवादी) perspective, an absolutist perspective, and the Reality or Truth

Ordinary Perspective

Often in our routine day-to-day lives, we barely give thought to our perspective. Not only this but we rarely think about the perspectives of those around us. When we see an object, an idea, or a situation we see it either as the Truth or the Reality. This is an ordinary view. Others may have the same ordinary view or may have a different or an absolutist view, yet it does not impact us because we are not aware of or interact with them. Generally, this does not create much conflict. Also, while we can all experience the truth we cannot verbalize it. For example, we can experience the sweetness of sugar but explaining it in words is difficult. Hence reality can be experienced but not completely expressed.

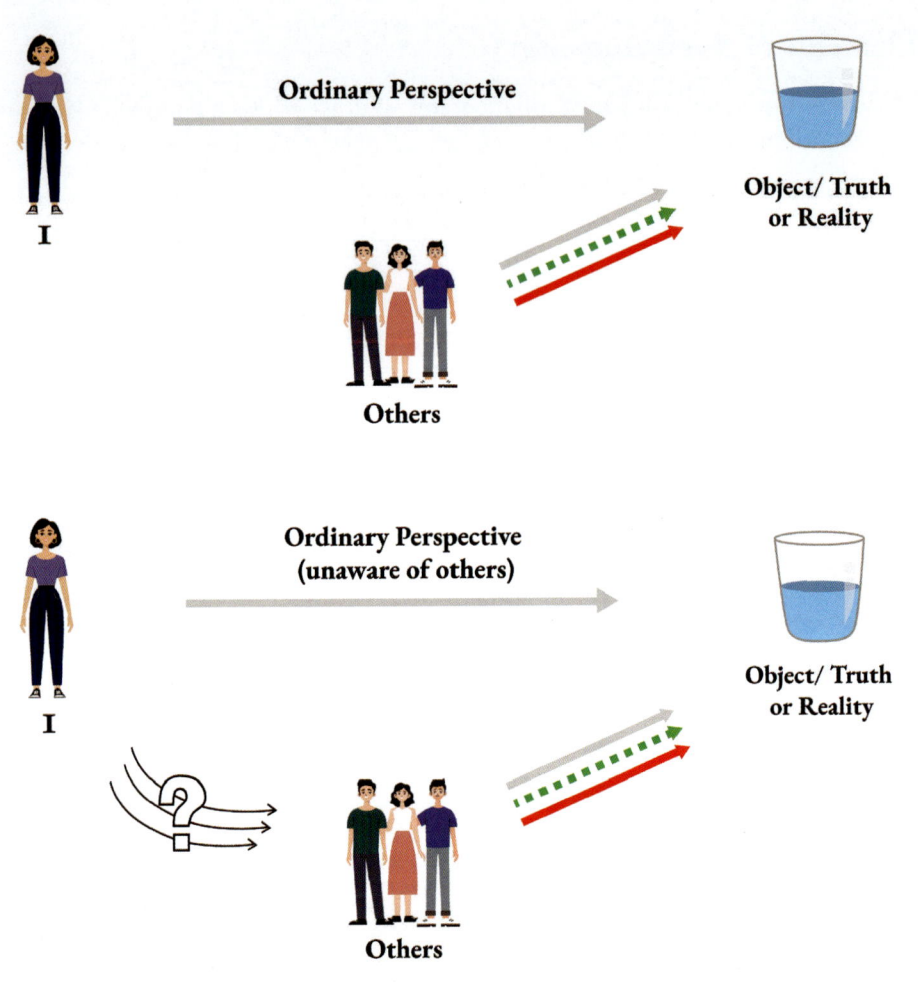

In the ordinary perspective of an object, we are unaware or unaffected by others' views.

Absolutist Perspective

With the passage of time and with persuasion, deep knowledge, and experience, we develop an Absolutist view of an object or Reality. When this happens the Absolutist self comes into conflict with others. The Absolutist self begins to reject and disrespect all other perspectives. These fundamental conflicts in the perspectives create unhappiness and conflict for all. The conflicts in perspective lead to baseless arguments, reasonless disputes, and environment harming violence.

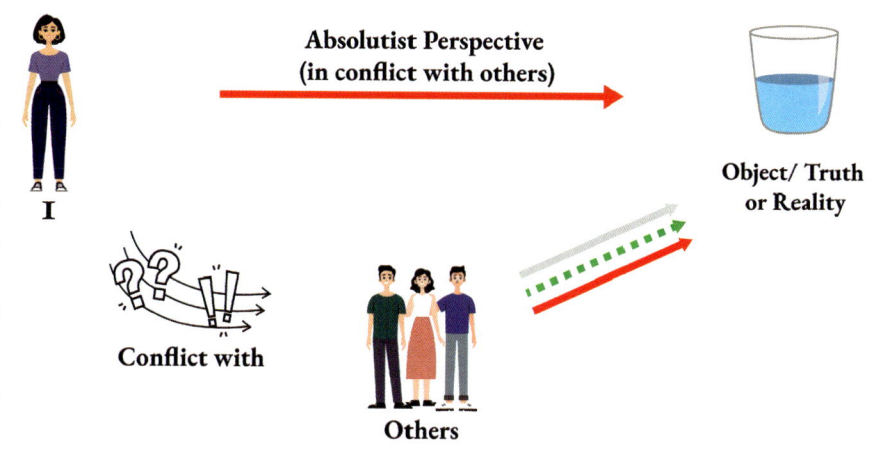

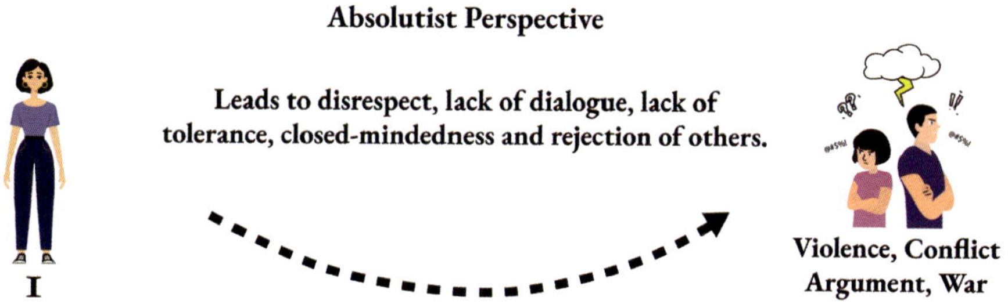

Absolutist perspective leads to violence and conflict with others

Jain Path

Anekantavada Perspective

When we have an *Anekantavada* view of an object, Reality or Truth, our *Anekantavada* self respects others and their views. We are tolerant. We dialogue with others. We are open-minded and accepting of others' views. The end result is that we respect others' views, and often others respect our views. Ultimately, this leads to avoidance of conflict, deepening of understanding, and ushers equanimity.

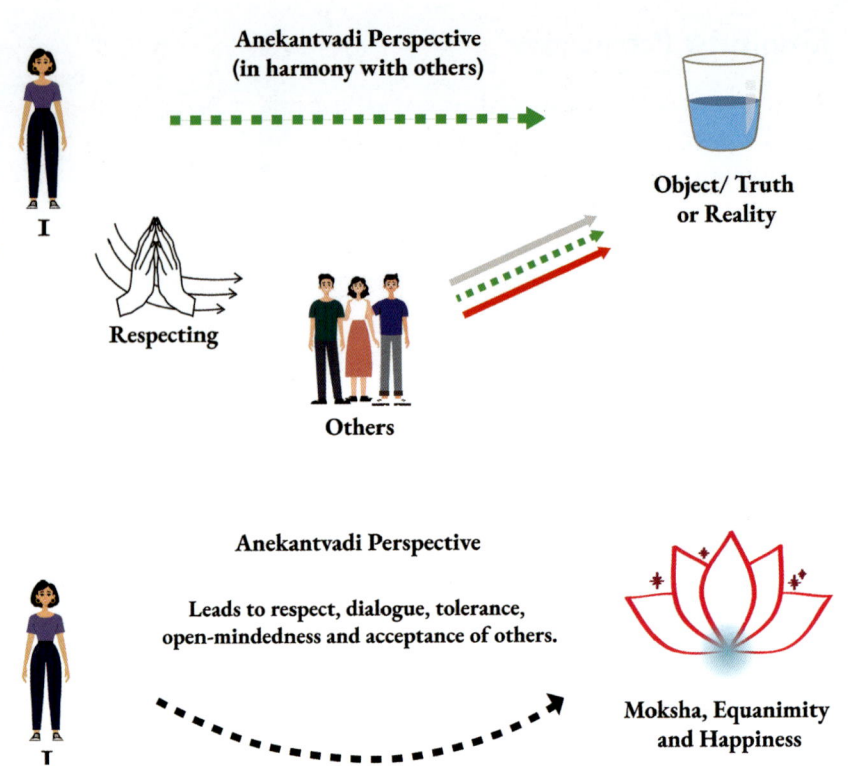

Anekantvadi perspective leads to respect and open-mindedness.

Jain sages have taken the principle of *Anekantavada* in further detail. If Reality (Truth) should not be perceived from an Absolute Perspective, then it can be perceived from the partial expression of truth (Naya). Jain sages describe this to be of two types: one that relates to a substance (*Nishchaya* - naya), and the other that relates to attributes or modes (*Vyvahar* naya). For instance, if we have a gold necklace, then the substance that it comes from is gold, which is eternal and unchanging or permanent (*Nishchaya*); on the other hand, the attribute form it takes is of a necklace which is ever-changing (*Vyavahar*). So, to better describe the necklace, we must use both the nischay and the *Vyavahar* perspective.

Jain sages take this principle to greater depths by introducing the concept of *syadvad,* or doctrine of relativity. The concept of *syadvad* or doctrine of relativity states that truth is relative to different viewpoints (*nayas*). What is valid from one point of view is open to question from another. Absolute truth cannot be grasped from any particular viewpoint alone because absolute truth is the sum total of all the different viewpoints that make up the universe.

Jainism and its principle of *Anekantavada* is a case-in-point against absolutism and fundamentalism that exists in the world today. Jainism does not look upon the universe from an anthropocentric (human-centric), ethnocentric (culture-centric), or egocentric (self-centered) viewpoint. In fact, it takes into account the viewpoints of other species, communities, nations, and human beings. Jains encourage dialog and harmony with other faiths.

Here is some food for thought! Read the questions given below, and ponder upon them with a calm and relaxed mind.
Are You a Fundamentalist?
Do you think you, your God, your scripture, or your view possesses the Truth?
Do you believe that someone possesses the Truth – the answer to everything?
Do you have a strict single-sided view of the past, present, and future?

A Jain would answer "no" to these questions. The fundamentalists would proclaim that their belief is infallible and that only they have the Truth. To reach their objectives, the fundamentalists supersede the wishes of others. He or she tramples the views of the majority of the people, hijacks the political process for their objectives, and uses any means, including violence or intimidation, to justify their ends.

Path to *Anekantavada* - Continuum of Views

There is a path we can follow to change from an Absolutist view to an Acceptance view. First, we need to know the different views.

Stage 1: Absolutist View – We believe that we have the Truth. Example: If a CEO of a business thinks in absolute terms, then his or her team tends to disengage. When views are either black or white, and there is no room for different opinions, this is an Absolutist view.

Stage 2: Tolerant View – We bear with and tolerate others' thoughts and ideas, yet we are arrogant and self-righteous about our own views. We do not take any steps to learn more about others' views.

Stage 3: Dialog View – We take active steps to explore the many perspectives that exist. This may include learning about others' faiths and interacting with new people. Here, we take the perspective that "I have a view, yet I wish to explore other's views."

Stage 4: Open-mindedness View – Belief that not only my view or one view is the correct view, but rather that there is a collage of views that lead to the Truth. Here, we take the perspective that "I have a view, and it may not be the most correct, and I am willing to listen to others' views."

Stage 5: Acceptance View – Acceptance of all perspectives and a humble respect for differences in beliefs. However, acceptance does not mean agreement with all the views; one can believe in only one faith and still have an accepting view of other faiths. Acceptance is not imposing your views on others, even if you believe your view is closer to Truth.

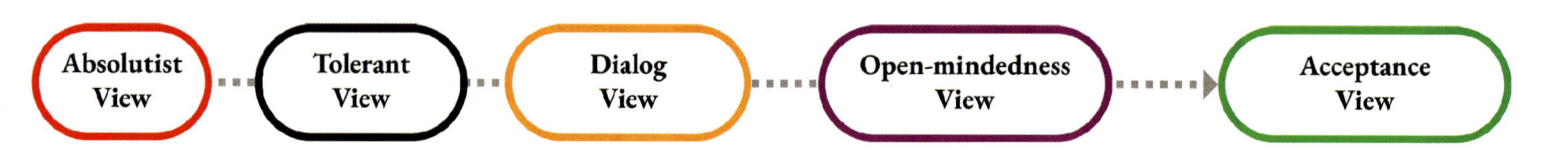

Absolutist View → Tolerant View → Dialog View → Open-mindedness View → Acceptance View

Path to Anekantavada - continuum of views

Anekantavada does not mean Agreement with other's views:

We can be tolerant, have a dialogue, be open-minded, or even accept another view; however, *Anekantavada* does not mean that we have to agree with all other views. Just as we cannot agree with someone who repeatedly commits acts of violence, though we may understand why they are doing it similarly, *Anekantavada* leads us to open-mindedness, hence leading us to acceptance of views.

The importance of this cannot be overemphasized since many who learn about *Anekantavada* think that it is perfectly alright to agree with all other views. Also, it does not mean we do not make an effort to help others see our view or a view that may be closer to the truth.

The parable of the six blind men illustrates the principle of *Anekantavada* in our daily lives.

The Parable of Blind Men and the Elephant

by John Godfrey Saxe

American poet John Godfrey Saxe (1816-1887) based the following poem on a Jain fable that was told in India centuries ago.

It was six men of Indostan To learning much inclined,
Who went to see the Elephant (Though all of them were blind), That each by observation
Might satisfy his mind
The First approached the Elephant, And happening to fall
Against his broad and sturdy side, At once began to bawl:
"God bless me! but the Elephant Is very like a wall!"
The Second, feeling of the tusk, Cried, "Ho! What have we here
So very round and smooth and sharp?
To me 'tis mighty clear This wonder of an Elephant
Is very like a spear!"
The Third approached the animal, And happening to take
The squirming trunk within his hands, Thus boldly up and spake:
"I see," quoth he, "the Elephant
Is very like a snake!"
The Fourth reached out an eager hand, And felt about the knee.
"What most this wondrous beast is like Is mighty plain," quoth he;

"'To me it is clear enough the Elephant Is very like a tree!"
The Fifth, who chanced to touch the ear, Said: "E'en the blindest man
Can tell what this resembles most; Deny the fact who can
This marvel of an Elephant Is very like a fan!"
The Sixth no sooner had begun About the beast to grope,

Than, seizing on the swinging tail That fell within his scope,
"I see," quoth he, "the Elephant Is very like a rope!"

Six blind men and an elephant

And so these men of Indostan Disputed loud and long, Each in his own opinion Exceeding stiff and strong, Though each was partly in the right, And all were in the wrong!

Transformation: How Do We Become Open-Minded?

Step 1: Stop and acknowledge that other views exist

Step 2 : Listen to and learn other's views

Step 3 : Respect and accept all views

Becoming aware and knowing that different perspectives exist may be simple, yet transforming oneself to be open-minded and accepting of the views of others is difficult.

The transformation process to be more open-minded and accepting has three major steps.

To Stop and to acknowledge means that we shift and change our ordinary unaware perspective of living. Often in our lives, we do not stop to think about the origins of our own beliefs and opinions. Through reflection, we achieve awareness of our own views, and this allows us to acknowledge the fact that, like us, others also have views.

To Listen and to Learn allows us to begin exploring the views of others, which we would not have done otherwise. Listening, reading, and watching is how we learn about the thoughts, ideas, feelings, and experiences of others. It helps us move out of our own single-minded thinking. Learning from others, not just listening, is essential. Learning means incorporating the views of others and recognizing the truth in their perspective.

To Accept and to Respect means to accept the other's view as their own. It means that we allow for diverse views to exist in one universe and see them as partial truths. Respecting means we provide space for others to express their views, and allow others to be able to share in an open dialogue respectfully without criticism or insult. Acceptance does not mean agreement. It opens the door for respectful exchange.

Jain sages were clear in their insistence on a worldview. From the *Tatttvartha Sutra* 1.33 (तत्वार्थ सूत्र verse 1.33), the following lines emphasize the same:

A person without an enlightened worldview is like an insane person who follows arbitrary whims and cannot distinguish true from false.

"The question then is: do I have an enlightened worldview?"

असदभिधानमनृतम् ॥ ७.१४ ॥

asadabhidhānamanṛtam ॥ 7.14 ॥

To speak what is not true is falsehood

-Tattvarth Sutra

APARIGRAHA (NONPOSSESSIVENESS)

Aparigraha (अपरिग्रह) *Nonpossessiveness*

Sharing material possessions, balance of needs and desires

Jain sages realized that excessive possessions are an obstruction in our path to happiness, equanimity, and moksha, just like violence and human mental conflict. Just as the sages provided an antidote for violence as nonviolence and for human mental conflict as Nonabsolutism, they provided an antidote for possessions too. It is *Aparigraha* or Nonpossessiveness.

Let's consider some basic questions to get a clear understanding of the concept of *Aparigraha*. What is possessiveness and Nonpossessiveness? What is the root cause of our possessiveness? What should we be nonpossessive towards? Why are possessions a hindrance to our spiritual journey? How can we practice the principle of Nonpossessiveness? The sages provide an answer to these fundamental questions.

To address the question of possessiveness and Nonpossessiveness one needs to review who is the "I."

We define the I as

I = **Self** *(soul)* + **Me** *(mind/body)* + **My** *(emotions/possessions - anger, money)* + **Us** *(family, friends)* + **Our** *(nation, world)*

In Jainism, the true Self is the Soul, and Everything else is the Other or (*Par* -पर) This includes the ME, which is the mind and the body; the MY, which is emotions and possession; the US, which is family and friends, and OUR which is nations and the world. Everything in the Other (*par*) are possessions we have during our lifetime. It is all this that will leave the Self when we die. The principle of *Aparigraha* teaches us how to live with possessions and how to use them towards our path to happiness, equanimity, and *moksha* (मोक्ष).

What is Nonpossessiveness?

Ancient Jain Sages realized that just as it was not possible to practice absolute nonviolence as a layperson, likewise, it is not possible to practice complete Nonpossessiveness. Possessiveness is a spectrum ranging from basic needs to necessities, comforts, wants, and finally to greed (*Lobh* लोभ).

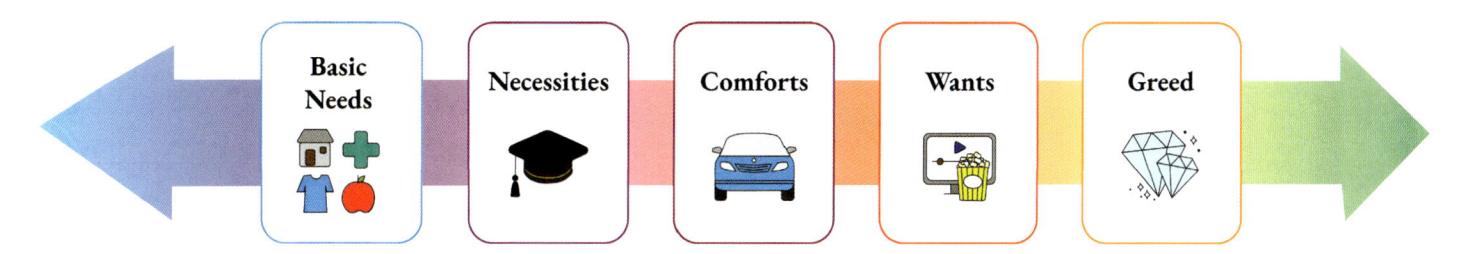

[Basic Needs → Necessities → Comforts → Wants → Greed]

The modern minimalist movement, with its focus on decluttering and intentional living, resonates with the principle of *Aparigraha* from Jainism. While minimalism in contemporary contexts often emphasizes environmental conservation, reducing economic burdens, and debt management, the Jain principle of *Aparigraha* serves a different purpose. In Jainism, the objective of minimizing possessions is deeply rooted in the idea of lessening one's karmic burden. By practicing non-attachment to material possessions, individuals seek to minimize the accumulation of karmas, which are believed to bind the soul to the cycle of birth and death.

Additionally, the concept of *Aparigraha* in Jainism underscores the understanding that genuine happiness and contentment are not inherently linked to material possessions or emotional gratification. Instead, the focus is on cultivating a sense of inner peace and spiritual fulfillment through detachment from the transient and ever-changing nature of material possessions. This differs from the contemporary minimalist movement's emphasis on simplifying life for practical and environmental reasons, highlighting the distinctive spiritual and karmic dimensions of *Aparigraha* within Jainism.

By recognizing the parallels and distinctions between the modern minimalist movement and the Jain principle of *Aparigraha*, individuals can gain a deeper understanding of the multifaceted nature of intentional living practices. While contemporary minimalism often addresses tangible aspects of lifestyle, Jainism offers a profound spiritual perspective, inviting reflection on the interconnectedness of material possessions, emotional well-being, and karmic implications. Through this understanding, individuals can explore the potential for a more holistic and balanced approach to minimalism, integrating both practical and spiritual considerations into their pursuit of simplicity and contentment.

Jain Path

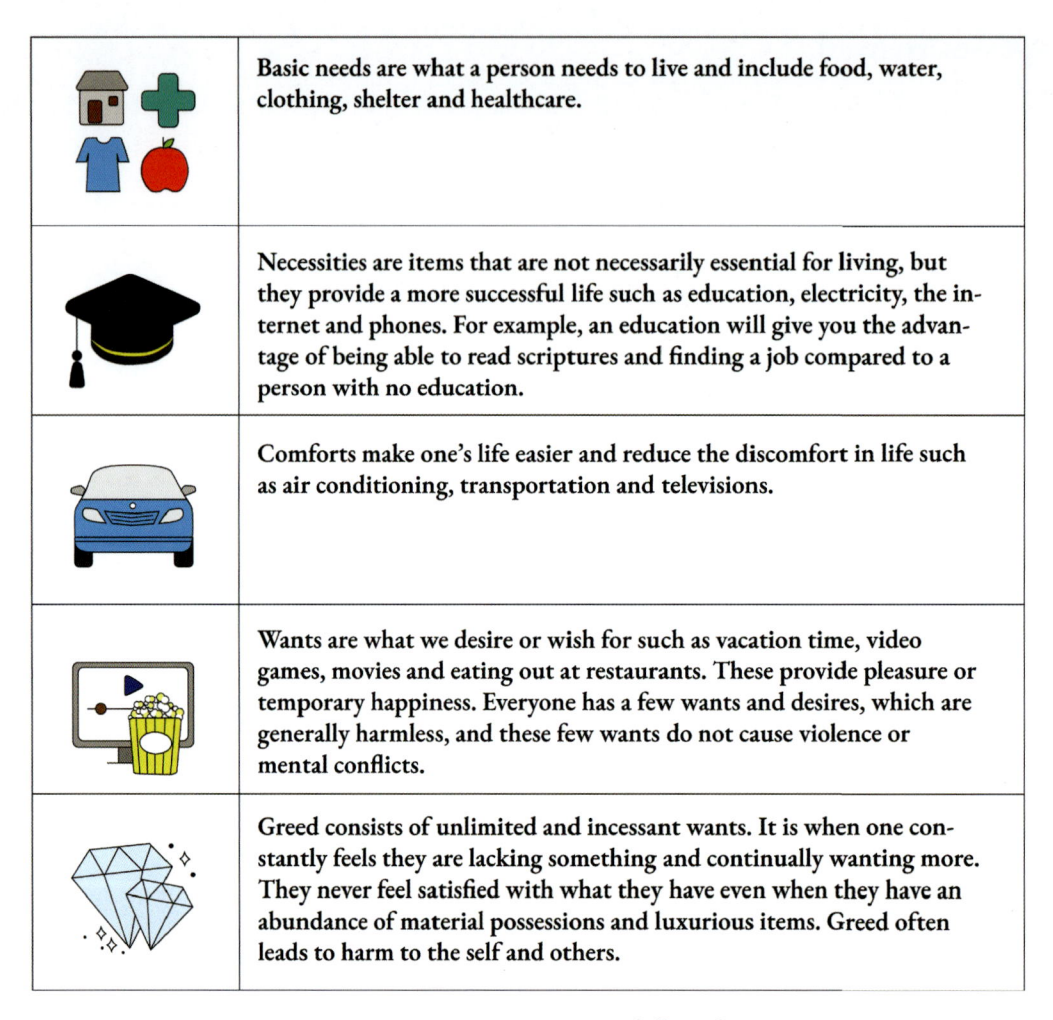

	Basic needs are what a person needs to live and include food, water, clothing, shelter and healthcare.
	Necessities are items that are not necessarily essential for living, but they provide a more successful life such as education, electricity, the internet and phones. For example, an education will give you the advantage of being able to read scriptures and finding a job compared to a person with no education.
	Comforts make one's life easier and reduce the discomfort in life such as air conditioning, transportation and televisions.
	Wants are what we desire or wish for such as vacation time, video games, movies and eating out at restaurants. These provide pleasure or temporary happiness. Everyone has a few wants and desires, which are generally harmless, and these few wants do not cause violence or mental conflicts.
	Greed consists of unlimited and incessant wants. It is when one constantly feels they are lacking something and continually wanting more. They never feel satisfied with what they have even when they have an abundance of material possessions and luxurious items. Greed often leads to harm to the self and others.

Jain scriptures encourage us to limit one's possession (*parimita-parigrah* परिमित परिग्रह) and limit one's desires or excessive wants (*iccha-parigraha* इच्छा परिग्रह).

What is the root cause of our possessiveness?

Sages teach us that it is not the possessions but Attachment (*raga* - राग) and Aversion (*dvesh* - द्वेष) that obstruct our path to happiness or incur karmic bondage. It is not the violence that causes the obstruction in the path of happiness or karmic bondage, but it is the Intention behind the violence. Every time the soul has an encounter with the other (*par* - पर) it develops a feeling of Attachment or Aversion, such as an attachment to a beautiful face and an aversion to cancerous growth. These Attachments and Aversions are the root source of possessiveness.

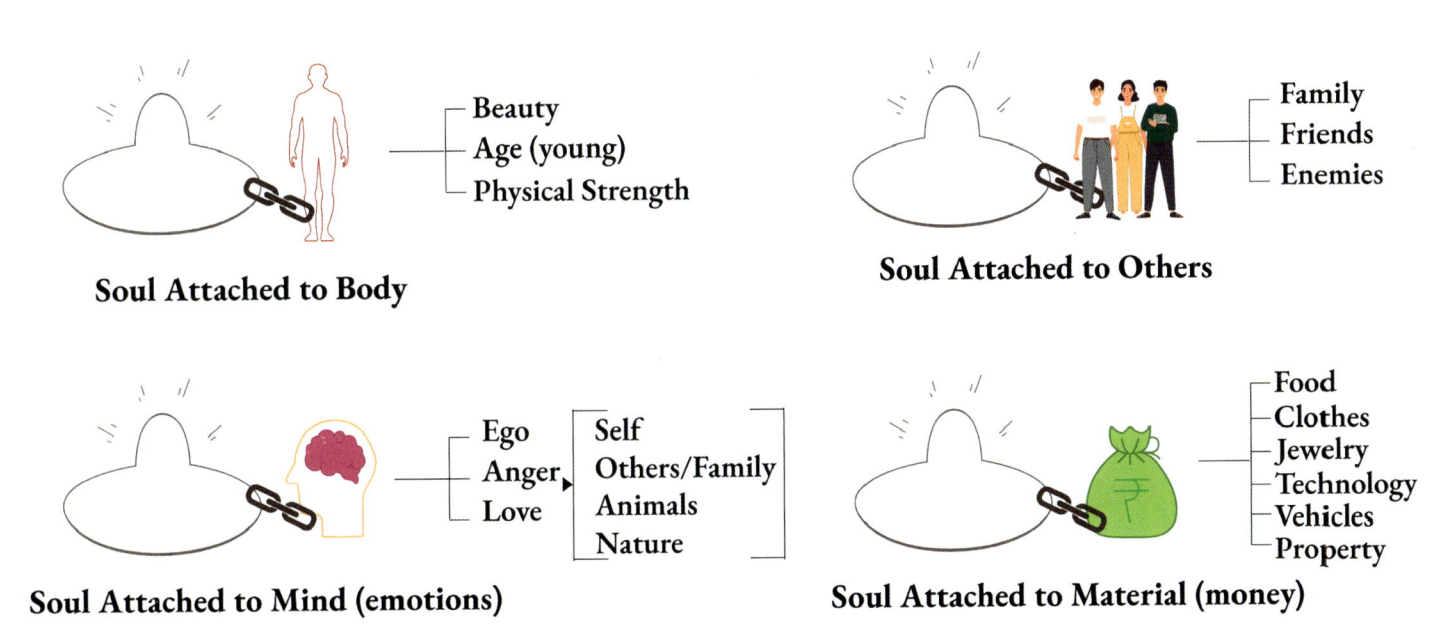

Soul Attached to Body
- Beauty
- Age (young)
- Physical Strength

Soul Attached to Others
- Family
- Friends
- Enemies

Soul Attached to Mind (emotions)
- Ego
- Anger → Self / Others/Family / Animals / Nature
- Love

Soul Attached to Material (money)
- Food
- Clothes
- Jewelry
- Technology
- Vehicles
- Property

Attachment and aversion to body, mind, people and materials

What should we be Nonpossessive towards?

Our Attachments and Aversion to objects, people, and even our own emotions lead to possessiveness. So we need to be nonpossessive towards them, and we need not have attachment or aversion towards:

- The Mind: our own ego, emotions of anger, love, jealousy, and greed.
- The Body: our beauty, disgustingness, youthfulness, old age, muscular strength, or physical frailty.
- Other People: our family, friends, and enemies
- Material Possessions: food, clothing, jewelry, technology, vehicles, property, money, and other objects.

In great detail Jain scriptures describe 24 types of possessions, some of which relate to ancient times. They include 14 internal possessions, such as anger and ego, and 10 external possessions, such as money and family.

Why are possessions a hindrance to our spiritual journey, and how can we practice the principle of Nonpossessiveness?

All the possessions, both material and nonmaterial, that come through attraction and aversion distract us from our spiritual path. Some, such as greed and jealousy, lead to harm to others. In the metaphysical sense, attraction and aversion lead to the influx and attachment of karma to the soul. Practicing nonpossessiveness requires us to avoid greed and wants. They are harmful to the self as well as others around us and even to the environment. A life with basic needs, necessities, and comforts is good. However, having possessions is not what is consequential; it is Attachment and Aversions we have in our day-to-day lives. So the sages guide us by mentioning that we need to have contentment (*samta bhava* समता भाव) to those outside of the self, may they be emotions, ideas, people, or materials. Contentment also averts karmic bondage.

How can we translate the principle of nonpossessiveness in our day-to-day life?

Ego	Acknowledge the ego, but do not allow it to seek attention or praise constantly.
Your Idea	Let go of your ideas and embrace different points of view.
Anger	Not being attracted or have aversion to anyone or anything - staying calm and tranquil.
Love (romantic)	Know that love is essential, yet allow the other person space and freedom.
Knowledge	Sharing knowledge with others, and mentoring and guiding them. Not being arrogant about one's own knowledg.
Faith	Deep understanding of one's faith but open to other ideas, discoveries, and facts.
Body	Understanding that body, beauty, intelligence, etc., are temporary and embracing change over time in the body. Also understanding that "my real nature is the soul.
Family	Loving and caring for all family members but allowing them their space over time and as new relationships form.
Enemies	Separate the action from the person. Do not have excessive aversion and revenge. Maintain calmness.
TV, Media, Internet, Games	Minimizing time and avoiding addiction with these time-consuming activities.
Material possessions such as Computers or Cars	Taking good care of one's material possessions but ready to share as needed and not becoming upset if you lose them or cannot purchase them.
Wealth	Donate a percentage of wealth for the spiritual benefits and material needs of others. Also, detach from ego when donating.
Life	Ready to embrace sickness and aging without anger, passion, and fear.

24 Jain Practices

AHIMSA

ANEKANTAVADA

APARIGRAHA

JAIN PRACTICES

What makes a person Jain? People may go to the temple yet eat meat regularly. They may believe in the Tirthankaras but not read any scriptures. Jainism is not just a philosophy or principles, but it is a way of life. Religiously following day to day practices which are derived from Jain Principles best describes a Jain person.

There are hundreds of Jain practices described in the scriptures. The *Tattvartha Sutra* chapter seven talks about the vows of the layperson, how one should be vegetarian and practice forgiveness and compassion. The *Acharanga Sutra* talks about the practice of humility and abandoning of ego over worldly things. However, some vows and practices require updating and reprioritizing for the modern day, such as *Tattvartha Sutra* verse 7.24/7.29, which talks about keeping "within the set limits of tillable land and buildings." Other vows require emphasis and prioritization, such as *Tattvartha Sutra* verse 7.6/7.11: "The observer of vows should cultivate friendliness towards all living beings." As well as the *Sutra* verse 5.21, "Souls render service to one another."

For the modern day, we can distill the many vows from the scriptures into 24 core practices. These practices are derived from the three core principles of *Ahimsa* (अहिंसा), *Anekantavada* (अनेकांतवाद), and *Aparigraha* (अपरिग्रह). Diligent and consistent activity (thought, speech, and action) of these vital practices can help us lead to a Jain Way of Life.

The first eight Jain practices are derived from the principle of Ahimsa. They relate to nonviolence towards others: Vegetarianism/Veganism, Forgiveness, Compassion, and Service. Also, they relate to nonviolence towards the Self: Yoga/Exercise, Carefulness, Intoxication Free and Stress Free.

The second eight Jain practices are derived from the principle of *Anekantavada*. They relate to our activity of thought, speech, and action in a non-absolutist manner. Being non-absolutist in Thought is Open-mindedness, Meditation/Mindfulness, and Respect. Being a non-absolutist in Speech is Humility and Straight-Forwardness, Being a non-absolutist in Action is Scripture reading, Equity, and Prayer/Pooja/Rituals.

The last eight Jain practices are derived from the principle of *Aparigraha*. This relates to Nonpossessiveness of the mind, body and social assets. Being nonpossessive of mind is Balancing our Needs and Wants, and Contentment. Being nonpossessive of the body is Fasting, Austerities, Controlling Sensual Desires, and Art of Dying. Being nonpossessive of societal assets is Charity and Environmentalism.

We can think of each Tirthankar as symbolizing one core practice, and by reciting their name we can recall the practice and then incorporate it into our lives.

AHIMSA PRACTICES

Vegetarian/Vegan/Jain Diet	Forgiveness	Compassion	Service
Yoga and Exercise	Carefulness	Intoxicant Free	Stress Free

AHIMSA PRACTICES
Nonviolence

Nonviolence Towards Others	**Vegetarian/Vegan/Jain Diet** - Promoting kindness and respect for other living beings through our diet. **Forgiveness** - Cultivating a mindset of understanding and compassion within ourselves and towards others, releasing anger and resentment. **Compassion** - Expressing empathy and love for others that goes beyond mere pity, sympathy, and empathy. **Service** - Demonstrating care and support for fellow humans and animals by providing assistance and help.
Nonviolence Towards Self	**Yoga and Exercise** - Nurturing a sense of well-being and self-care for our bodies through physical activities. **Carefulness** - Practicing mindfulness and avoiding unnecessary harm in thought, speech, and action, including refraining from criticizing or insulting others (Samitis - Guptis). **Intoxicant Free** - Maintaining a healthy and self-respecting lifestyle by abstaining from smoking, alcohol, and drugs. **Stress Free** - Promoting peace and well-being for oneself and one's family by ensuring adequate rest and sleep.

Nonviolence Practices

Vegetarian/Vegan/Jain Diet - Promoting kindness and respect for other living beings through our diet.

We are what we eat, and so we must partake in food that is derived from the most nonviolent means. Fruits, vegetables, and grains cause the least violence and are most beneficial for our health and well-being. The Jain principle of nonviolence leads to healthy eating. Going beyond a vegetarian diet is a vegan diet where we avoid any harm that is done when milk is procured. A Jain diet of avoiding root vegetables reduces further harm to an entire plant.

The practice of being vegetarian and vegan leads to a healthy body and a healthy mind.

In Tattvartha Sutra verse 7.30/7.35, Eating animate food, eating things in contact with animate food, eating things mixed with animate food, eating half-cooked food are transgressions.

Jain scripture of Dasha Vaikalika Sutra states "All living creatures desire to live. Nobody wishes to die." A clear reference to a vegetarian diet is through the principle of ahimsa.

A vegetarian and vegan practice not only leads us to live a compassionate and nonviolent life, but it is economical, healthy, and environmentally sound. One can achieve a well-rounded and balanced spiritual health along with keeping away from fatal life conditions like obesity, heart attacks, and cancer with a vegetarian/vegan diet. Not only this, but vegetarianism also aids us in reducing our carbon footprint.

Forgiveness - Cultivating a mindset of understanding and compassion within ourselves and towards others, releasing anger and resentment.

Keeping anger (*krodh* क्रोध - a kashya कषाय) is a form of mental violence. Jains celebrate a day of forgiveness during *paryushan* (पर्यूषण) and do *pratikraman* (प्रतिक्रमण) as a way to overcome anger and seek forgiveness.

One key ingredient to happiness is unconditional forgiveness. The practice of Forgiveness is derived from the nonviolence of the mind toward others and oneself. Forgiveness is critical in the practice of nonviolence in transforming our thoughts, speech, and actions to equanimity and harmony.

Jain scriptures emphasize Forgiveness as a vow and practice.

In Tattvartha Sutra verse 7.6/7.11, scriptures ask one to make the famous scriptural resolve: "I forgive all creatures. I cultivate friendliness with all. I harbor resentment against none."

Tattvartha Sutra 9.6 gives the Description of 10 Dharmas: Morality is perfect forgiveness...

Forgiveness has two components. First is to ask for forgiveness, and second is to give forgiveness to others. Asking for forgiveness is so essential that it is the central aspect of the Jain ritual *Pratikraman*. In *Pratikraman*, we ask for forgiveness from all living beings. By asking for forgiveness, we reduce clinging to a moment, an incident, or an event that keeps repeating in our minds. By forgiving others, we reduce our anger, depression, and stress. We also become more hopeful, peaceful, compassionate, and confident. In the end, our relationships grow stronger.

Scientific literature today shows the physical, mental, and emotional benefits of forgiving others. Research studies show that acts of forgiveness lead to a lower risk of heart attack, improved cholesterol levels, better sleep, less pain, lower blood pressure, and less anxiety, depression, and stress.

Compassion - Expressing empathy and love for others that goes beyond mere pity, sympathy, and empathy.

The highest form of nonviolence is to take action to relieve the suffering of others. When another person or any living creature is suffering, we can respond in one of four ways. The first type of response is to have pity, which is to have sorrow for another with no desire to intervene. The second type of response to suffering is to have sympathy, which is to have sorrow and a desire to do something to relieve the suffering but not have the ability to do so. The third type of response to suffering is to have empathy. This is to have sorrow so deep that you feel as if the pain is your own. The last type of response to suffering is Compassion, which is to have such a strong desire to relieve the sorrow of another that one takes some form of action to alleviate others' suffering.

Jains practice compassion towards others and all living beings, and it is derived from the principle of Ahimsa. Whether it is donating food and clothes to the needy around us or following vegetarianism to avoid harm to animals, the practice of compassion for others is a central thought in Jainism.

Jain Scriptures emphasize compassion as one of four bhavanas or reflections.

In Tattvartha Sutra verse 7.6/7.11 it states, " The observer of vows should cultivate friendliness towards all living beings ... compassion for miserable, lowly creatures..." Jainism is a religion of compassion. Tattvartha Sutra states 6.13/6.12 "Compassion through charity for all living beings and purity (freedom from greed) causes the inflow of pleasure karma."

In our daily lives, it is essential that we bring warmth, love, and kindness through our thoughts, speech, and actions. Scientific literature shows us that compassion and kindness increase our self-esteem, improve our mood, decrease our blood pressure, and lower our stress cortisol levels. In addition, compassion boosts good hormones such as serotonin and dopamine in our brain and increases endorphins which are our body's natural pain killers.

Service - Demonstrating care and support for fellow humans and animals by providing assistance and help.

Service is an action taken by an individual which helps another. Service can be done for material gain (money), or it can be done for no material gain, no fame, or not even recognition. The greatest service is when it is done with no expectations of reciprocation. Providing service or money that is more than necessary or more than expected is generosity. The positive aspect of nonviolence is providing service or generosity to others. Services a doctor, a waitress or a philanthropist provides are services that Jainism encourages.

Jain scriptures' most famous quote is from *Tattvartha Sutra 5.21, which says Parasparopagraho jivanam "Souls render services to one another."* This quote defines the function of souls in the world. Though souls are striving for liberation, they "influence each other through service which may be favorable or unfavorable, beneficial or harmful. They cannot live independently of one another. They have to share their pleasure and pain with others. As partners in good and evil acts, they are jointly responsible, although they must bear the karmic results individually for the part they play. They create a common environment and live together in weal and woe." *Tattvartha Sutra 6.23* describes the 16 virtues of the Jain Path, including service to others, such as monks and nuns.

Service towards others is good for our health. Scientific studies show that Generosity in particular, leads to greater happiness. Helping others while on the job boosts happiness at work, improves well-being, and makes us more committed to work. Other studies published in the American Journal of Public Health showed that being generous and selfless leads to a lower risk of early death.

Yoga and Exercise - Nurturing a sense of well-being and self-care for our bodies through physical activities.

Doing exercise and practicing yoga makes our body, mind, and emotions healthy and fit. The Jain principle of nonviolence to our bodies leads to this practice. We must be nonviolent to our own bodies to be healthy and fit both physically and emotionally.

The ancient scriptures do not directly talk about daily physical exercise or the practice of yoga; however, they encourage the well-being of the body for the well-being of the mind.

We often do not realize the benefits of fitness of the body, which leads to the fitness of the mind, which in turn leads our souls to take the path of liberation. One can begin with simple mindful stretching exercises every day or mindful, peaceful walking in the morning or evening. Present-day spiritual leaders encourage the practice of yoga and exercise. During exercise, one needs to keep the mind focused on the movement. This helps the mind be tranquil from disturbing thoughts as well as derive maximum benefit from the exercises. Yoga and Exercise are not just a physical activity but a spiritual activity.

Tattvartha Sutra States: 6.1 The action of the body, the speech organ and the mind is called yoga (activity). 6.2 These three types of yoga cause vibration/throbbing in the space points of the soul resulting in influx (asrava) i.e. incoming of karmas.

Today, there are many well-done scientific studies that show the benefit of yoga to our bodies and minds. A detailed article from Johns Hopkins Medicine outlines 9 benefits of yoga: strengthening balance and flexibility, relieving back pain, easing arthritis symptoms, benefiting heart health, relaxing and improving sleep, improving energy and mood, managing stress, connecting with a supportive community, and better self-care.

Carefulness - Practicing mindfulness and avoiding unnecessary harm in thought, speech, and action, including refraining from criticizing or insulting others. (*Samitis - Guptis*)

We can inflict harm in many ways, knowingly and unknowingly. To avoid harm, one must actively practice Carefulness. If one practices the Carefulness of the mind, it leads to the carefulness of speech, which in turn leads to the carefulness of one's action. Carefulness is a practice derived from the principle of nonviolence.

The Jain scriptures emphasize carefulness in the forms of *Samitis* and *Guptis*. For example, there are *samitis* that describe carefulness in the regulation of walking, speaking, seeking food, laying down articles, and disposal of waste. Also, there are *Guptis* or regulation of mind, speech, and bodily action.

Tattvartha Sutra States: 9.4 Guarding through body, speech and mind. 9.5 To move carefully is to walk, speak, seek alms, handle objects of daily use and dispose of excreta in the correct manner.

Today, Good moral conduct, good business practices, good workplace behavior as well as good school-based behavior emphasize that one must lead a life that keeps the feelings of others in mind. Harm is determined as much by the intention of the action as by the impact that it causes on the other person. Carefulness is the best practice in our society, where every moment is an interaction with another person and impacts the lives of other living beings.

Intoxicant Free - Maintaining a healthy and self-respecting lifestyle by abstaining from smoking, alcohol, and drugs.

Intoxicants such as tobacco, alcohol, and illicit drugs are ubiquitous in present society and have been part of society for millennia. Sages and modern scientists both agree that intoxicants are harmful to the self. The practice of an Intoxicant free life is derived from the principle of avoiding harm or nonviolence toward one's own body and mind.

Drinking alcohol is denounced in ancient Jain texts. The Purushartha Siddhi-Upaya states, "Alcohol stupefies the mind; one whose mind is stupefied forgets piety; and one who forgets piety commits violence without hesitation."

The Tattvartha Sutra verse 7.30 lists "drinking alcohol" as one of the transgressions of the vows.

According to the US Department of Health & Human Services Department of Substance Abuse and Mental Health Services Administration, "misusing alcohol, tobacco and other drugs can have both immediate and long-term health effects. Excessive alcohol leads to a person's risk of stroke, liver cirrhosis, alcoholic hepatitis, and cancer. Also, in the United States, 29 people die each day in motor vehicle crashes due to alcohol. Tobacco is the leading cause of preventable death in the USA, causing 480,000 deaths each year and 16 million Americans living with diseases caused by tobacco. Drug overdose leads to 129 deaths each day in the USA and puts millions of people at risk for HIV and Hepatitis B and C.

Stress-Free - Promoting peace and well-being for oneself and one's family by ensuring adequate rest and sleep.

Stress is present in daily life. Stress is a physical, mental, and emotional feeling that comes from a change or conflict. If stress is not dealt with in an appropriate manner, it negatively impacts the self, the family, and the community. Stress is caused by overwork, self-criticism, and negative thoughts.

Jain scriptures recognize the impact of stress. The scriptures encourage "*Samta*" which means that one must maintain one's composure in favorable and unfavorable conditions. Moreover, the Theory of Karma provides answers as to why "bad things" happen. Such philosophical understanding allows a Jain person to cope with stress at the most challenging times.

Tattvartha Sutra States: 9.27 Focus on single object is meditation which leads to less stress 9.31 to 9.34/9.30 to 9.33 Describes about getting rid of disagreeable objects, unhappy situations, unpleasant feelings and intense anxiety.

Stress is unhealthy for the body and the mind. Stress leads to anxiety, anger, depression, poor memory, heart problems, more infections, muscle tension, headaches, weight gain, and insomnia. Many other Jain practices, such as meditation, forgiveness, and prayer, directly impact to reduce stress. Rituals and routine religious activity decrease the stressful time periods in a day and increase the calm and tranquil moments.

ANEKANTAVADA PRACTICES

| Open-mindedness | Meditation and Mindfulness | Respect | Humility |

| Straight-forwardness | Scripture Reading | Equity | Prayer-Pooja |

ANEKANTAVADA PRACTICES
Nonabsolutism

Nonabsolutism of Thought	**Open-Mindedness** - Embracing the diversity of perspectives, including our own, and maintaining a receptiveness to multiple viewpoints, avoiding rigid or dogmatic thinking. **Meditation and Mindfulness** - Cultivating an open and flexible mindset by engaging in self-reflection and self-awareness without rigidly clinging to thoughts. **Respect** - Nurturing an attitude of openness and acceptance in our relationships, fostering tolerance and understanding of other's viewpoints.
Nonabsolutism of Speech	**Humility** - Recognizing that we do not need to constantly seek the spotlight and letting go of ego-driven behaviors. **Straight-forwardness** - Avoiding deceit, being transparent and honest in our interactions, and seeking to understand the perspectives of others.
Nonabsolutism of Action	**Scripture Reading** - Embracing a flexible approach to our beliefs and actively seeking knowledge about our own faith as well as the beliefs of others. **Equity** - Embracing fairness and impartiality in our treatment of people, regardless of their race, religion, ethnicity, or status, and refraining from stereotypes, biases, prejudices, or discrimination. **Prayer** - Demonstrating commitment to positive thoughts and actions through our daily practices without being rigid or dogmatic.

Nonabsolutism Practices

Open-mindedness - Embracing the diversity of perspectives, including our own, and maintaining a receptiveness to multiple viewpoints, avoiding rigid or dogmatic thinking.

We can see the world from an absolutist view, a tolerant view, or a dialog view. These are all default perspectives or lenses through which we see the world. We need to reject the other perspective and choose Open-mindedness as our perspective towards the world. While other perspectives limit our vision of the world and, in turn, the true reality of nature or the truth, open-mindedness opens doors. It is simply listening before speaking and not being biased or prejudiced towards others' perspectives.

Jain principle teaches us that we cannot have an absolute or a closed minded view.

In Tattvartha Sutra's 5.31/5.32 interpretation, Nathmal Tatia writes, " Jainism denies absolute existence or absolute non-existence, absolute permanence or absolute impermanence and defends nonabsolutism. Open-mindedness is the path to nonabsolutism.

While the philosophical construct of this practice and principle goes deep into the nature of reality and the nature of existence, the practice is simply listening without prejudices. The most novel and yet under-recognized treasure that Jainism offers the world is the practice of open-mindedness framed in the principle of nonabsolutism and the Triple A's. Corporate businesses are recognizing the importance of their senior leaders to be open-minded and being in a listening mode to their employees and their customers. Open-mindedness is encouraged at universities and colleges to help young people discover the virtues of other individuals and traditions. Open-mindedness has many practical benefits. It helps us gain insight, have new experiences, achieve personal growth, become mentally strong, feel more optimistic, and learn new things.

Meditation and Mindfulness - Cultivating an open and flexible mindset by engaging in self-reflection and self-awareness without rigidly clinging to thoughts.

The Jain principle of *Anekantavada* comes through self-awareness and self-reflection. The practice of meditation, a practice when the mind is clear of all thoughts, and a practice of mindfulness, when the mind is fully aware of all thoughts, leads to self-awareness

Meditation is a practice deeply rooted in Jain philosophy.

Tattvartha Sutra 9.27 describes meditation: "The concentration of thought on a single object by a person with good bone-joints is meditation."

Nathmal Tatia explains this in more detail. Meditation is the sixth sub-type of internal austerity, where the "restless mind moves from one object to another. It is immersed in thought. When the restless mind concentrates on a single object, it is meditating. This is a kind of restriction placed on the mind to steal it. The stilling of the speech organs and the body is also a type of meditation."

Tattvartha Sutra 9.28 defines that the meditative state lasts less than forty-eight minutes. "The meditative state lasts an intro-hour."

While the Jain religion has advocated the practice of meditation for over two millennia, science has only discovered meditation's benefits in the past several decades. Studies show without question that meditation reconfigures our brains, even adding additional gray matter, which are critical neurons that help us think and process information. Meditation can reduce stress, control anxiety, promote emotional health, enhance self-awareness, lengthen attention span, generate kindness, reduce addiction, improve sleep, control pain, and decrease blood pressure.

Respect - Nurturing an attitude of openness and acceptance in our relationships, fostering tolerance and understanding of others' viewpoints.

Jainism promotes respect not just for other human beings but for all creatures, small or large. Respect is an attitude of high regard towards another. Regard for another comes from relationships that need to be built and maintained. Respect is earned over time, it cannot be demanded or requested. The principle of *Anekantavada* relates to how relationships should be made, which is with respect to others' views. Respect requires one to raise others to their level and never to think that one is above others and that others are beneath them. We can take respect to a greater degree by showing our gratitude towards them. Gratitude is respect, humility, and thankfulness combined.

Jain scriptures hold high regard for respect, and the word is विनय *Vinay*. Respect is for parents, teachers, religious books, monks, and much more.

In Tattvartha Sutra 9.20, the second of six internal austerities are described as Reverence. "Reverence means due respect for learning and the learned." Sutra 9.23 describes further, "The four references are for learning, the enlightened world-view, good conduct and senior ascetics."

A simple way to show respect to others is to greet one another with Jai Jinendra. Our colleagues, parents, or children do not want money, material goods, or excessive praise from us but simply Respect. Business literature shows the benefits of respect in the workplace. Unfortunately, according to a study conducted by *Harvard Business Review,* half of employees do not feel respected by their bosses. Respect was found to be the single greatest leader behavior that impacted employees' outcomes, above recognition, appreciation, inspiring vision, useful feedback, and opportunities to learn and grow. Employees who felt respected had 90% greater job satisfaction.

Humility - Recognizing that we do not need to constantly seek the spotlight and letting go of ego-driven behaviors.

Humility is humbleness where one's own ego is not greater than that of others. The principle of *Anekantavada* helps us see the world from beyond the self and when our perspective equals that of another. Humble people do not actively seek unnecessary attention or excessive praise. Humble people greet and respect all others equally and do not distinguish those with money, fame, reputation, beauty, and power. In speech, a humble person uses less "I, me, and my" and more 'We, us, and our." Change in action for a humble person is uplifting others equally and beyond their level in different stages of their progress. A humble person's thoughts are different, too. They do not derive energy from public recognition but from personal individual respect and compassion towards others.

In Tattvartha Sutra 9.6, details are given of the third way to inhibit karmic inflow, which is through the ten moral virtues (also the 10 dharmas of the DasLakshan Dharma. "Morality is perfect forgiveness, humility, straight forwardness, purity from greed, truthfulness, self-restraint, austerity, renunciation, detachment and continence."

Nathmal Tatia describes this further. "Humility arises when pride about one's race, family, prosperity, intellect, knowledge, and other such attainments is subdued."

Humility is not just a good personal skill but a business and leadership skill. *Forbes Coaches Council* describes 17 reasons that humility will help you get ahead, which include curiosity, accountability, self-reflection, handling change, seeing beyond yourself, and earning admiration and respect.

Straight-Forwardness - Avoiding deceit, being transparent and honest in our interactions, and seeking to understand the perspectives of others.

In today's world, it is easy to manipulate facts, withhold information, or to sabotage a colleague's work. We can intentionally reach a false conclusion for personal gain. With so much data being available, we can manipulate it to support any view one wishes, and hence, we have political advertisements that leave many in conflict as to what to believe. News media do this to fit their agenda. Straightforwardness requires us to search deeply within ourselves and see if we are presenting the facts as they are and not in a deceitful or manipulative way. The principle of *Anekantavada* helps us in this practice because it allows us to reflect on others' perspectives.

In Tattvartha Sutra 9.6 the third morality is described as Straightforwardness. "Straightforwardness is sincere and honest intention…It is also avoiding controversy." Sutra 6.22: Straightforwardness attract beneficial Karma

In professional dealing, Straight-Forwardness is what earns the respect of our partners and clients. We can deceive others once, maybe twice, but not usually the third or fourth time. Corporations that build trust and respect by straightforwardness earn the greatest process. Trust is the single most valuable trait in a company with high trust. There is "106% greater energy in the office, 74% lower stress levels, 76% greater engagement, and 50% more productivity than their peers at low-trust businesses."

Scripture Reading - Embracing a flexible approach to our beliefs and actively seeking knowledge about our own faith as well as the beliefs of others.

Scriptures offer a first-hand account of the words of sages, may they be that of Jesus, Buddha, Muhhamed, or Mahavira. The practice of reading the scriptures, such as the *Tattvartha Sutra*, provides a better understanding of one's own religion and that of other religions. Anekantavada does not require us to accept the teachings in other scriptures; however, it requires us to be aware of those teachings and respect them.

In Tattvartha Sutra 9.20 the third of six internal austerities is described as "scripture study." In Sutra 9.25 scripture reading is further detailed. "The five stages of scripture study are: teaching, questioning, reflection, correct recitation and preaching of the doctrine." In Sutra 6.14/6.13 Scripture for right worldview; 6.23/6.24 Scriptures lead to Jina Path

Scriptures often make a person more religious. Scientific studies done on people who are religious find they tend to be healthier and live longer due to social support and a sense of purpose in life.

Equity - Embracing fairness and impartiality in our treatment of people, regardless of their race, religion, ethnicity, or status, and refraining from stereotypes, biases, prejudices, or discrimination.

Equity refers to the qualities of justness, fairness, impartiality, and even-handedness, while equality is about equal sharing and exact division. Equality refers to equalness in quantity, whereas equity means equalness in the end outcome. We live in a complex world where often, in our daily interactions, we are forced to make split-second decisions. Should I buy something, meet someone, or talk with someone? To ease the decision, our mind generalizes, which comes in various forms: stereotyping, prejudice, bias, and discrimination. Stereotyping is generalizing a group of people. Prejudice is prejudging others based on the group. Bias is having an unreasoned and unfair distortion often based on prejudgement. Lastly, discrimination is actual unfair treatment based on biases.

Jain scriptures talk of equity in the broadest of terms and as a guiding value.

Tattvartha Sutra 7.1 states: Vows on equity of living beings, perspectives, and basic needs

Equity of the three Jain principles of Ahimsa, *Anekantavada* and *Aparigraha* is equity of souls, equity of perspectives, equity of material possessions. In the opening paragraph of the translation of the *Tattvartha Sutra*, Nathmal Tatia talks about Nonviolence strengthening the morality and equalness of the soul, Nonabsolutism strengthening the morality and equality of thought, and Nonpossessiveness strengthening the morality and equality of interdependence of all existence.

In our daily professional and personal lives, we are becoming more equitable. Equity in gender, with women having the right to vote; equity in race, with the end of slavery and civil rights efforts; and equity in income, with the start of minimum wage. The human race needs to move forward with equity.

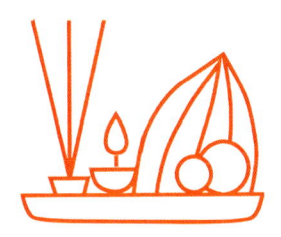

Prayer - Demonstrating commitment to positive thoughts and actions through our daily practices without being rigid or dogmatic.

The practice of Pooja or prayer is an act of bhakti, which in the Hindu traditions is considered one of the paths to salvation. It may be a morning prayer, evening pooja, daily bhajan, or abhishek at the temple. During a ritual, the mind, speech, and body become focused and calm. The rituals, over time, become so routine that the mind, too, comes into spiritual mode when the prayer and pooja begin. Emotional calmness sets in. Another ritual duty for Jains is to provide food and refuge for the ascetics.

Padmanabh Jaini writes that the Jain scriptures do not emphasize rituals however, "For most Jains, practicing their faith centers upon a diverse group of daily rituals and periodic ceremonies, many of which reflect the ideal lay path, but differ in that there is no compulsion attached. … Jain image worship must be understood as meditational; the icon is seen merely as an ideal, a state attainable by all embodied souls. There is no "deity" actually present. Since most ancient Jaina texts seem to make no reference to Jina images." However, Jaina texts do emphasize caring for ascetics.

Tattvartha Sutra 6.23/6.24 states among the sixteen karma leading to life of the Jina are "rendering service to the nuns and monks and pure devotion to the adorable one, pure devotion to the spiritual teacher, pure devotion to learned monks, pure devotion to the scripture."

The benefits of rituals and prayers are defined well in science. Research from Duke University shows that rituals reduce stress, leading to lower blood pressure. Also, religiosity, or the act of going to church, shows health benefits. When doing prayer, one inherently begins to feel peaceful and tranquil, and blood pressure and anger begin to come down.

APARIGRAHA PRACTICES

| Balancing Needs and Wants | Contentment | Fasting | Austerities |

| Controlling Sensual Desires | Art of Dying | Charity | Environmentalism |

APARIGRAHA PRACTICES
Nonpossessiveness

Nonpossessiveness of Mind	**Balancing Needs and Wants** - Cultivating a mindset free from attachment to our material needs, avoiding greed, and achieving equilibrium between necessities and desires. **Contentment** - Fostering a mental state devoid of possessiveness towards others' possessions, finding happiness in our own, and refraining from jealousy or comparisons with others.
Nonpossessiveness of Body	**Fasting** - Cultivating a mindset free from excessive attachment to food or desire for it, diminishing our preoccupation with consumption. **Austerities** - Practicing moderation and restraint in our engagement with the five senses, while engaging in *Tap/Tyag*. **Controlling Sensual Desires** - Exercising self-control and detachment from excessive longing for sensual pleasures, as reflected in *Sanyam* संयम. **Art of Dying** - Embracing a state of detachment and non-attachment to both the material world and the body.
Nonpossessiveness in Social Causes	**Charity** - Generously sharing one's wealth with others, free from attachment to money. **Environmentalism** - Embracing responsible resource usage and demonstrating care and respect for the Earth while refraining from personal possession of materials.

Nonpossessiveness Practices

Balancing Needs and Wants - Cultivating a mindset free from attachment to our material needs, avoiding greed, and achieving equilibrium between necessities and desires.

There is a delicate balance of how one may define what is a "need" and what is a "want." What is critical is how one defines this for oneself. In an act of self-reflection, if we define our needs and wants, then we can more clearly identify when our needs will end, and our wants will begin. The needs and wants may be related to the number of cars, size of a house, amount of jewelry in the safe, money in the bank, or stocks in our portfolio. A spectrum exists of basic needs, necessities, comforts, wants, and greed. The Jain principle of *Aparigraha* encourages us to balance our needs and recognize that happiness is not derived from materials but through equanimity.

Tattvartha Sutra 9.26 states, "Renunciation means abandoning the external articles and the internal passions including the body." Renunciation includes material possessions. While laypersons, it is not expected to renounce all material objects, it is always better to minimize our possessions. Often, it is not having the possessions but the attachment to possessions that causes our anger and distress.

Tattvartha Sutra 7.16/7.21 states, "The seven supplementaries which enrich the observer of the small vows are: … limiting the use of consumable and non-consumable goods…" And refers to *"food, drink, cosmetics, rich clothes, and jewelry, beds, chairs, vehicles, and so on."* 7.4l(7.5 to 7.9) talks of Avoid Greed and anger 7.27 limit excessive use of consumer goods

The scientific literature and life coaches emphasize balancing our life between professional and personal lives, in work and play, as well as money and time. Finding this balance is critical if one is to live a happy life. There is no escaping such a balance in life. The balance should be driven by us and our own expectations of ourselves and not that of others around us.

Contentment - Fostering a mental state devoid of possessiveness towards others' possessions, finding happiness in our own, and refraining from jealousy or comparisons with others.

Material things surround us, and the old adage holds true: "Earth provides enough to satisfy every man's needs, but not enough for one man's greed." Also, we live in a world of comparisons. Outright jealousy or subtle envy are thought to be natural, normal human emotions. Such is not the case. Jealousy, envy, and even greed arise from one's own sense of insecurity. An unaware person is often too lost in their own self. They do not realize that the pain of jealousy and unmet greed is being generated by their mind and that it can be extinguished by it. We only need to make an effort to do so.

In Tattvartha Sutra 8.10/8.9, the deluding karmas are, among others, the "four passions of anger, pride, deceit, and greed." The antidote to greed is described in 9.6 as "purity (freedom from greed)," or contentment. The greedy mind is "always impure… the mind-polluting passions produced by greed as anger, pride, deceit, violence."

Contentment is beneficial for the body and mind. It relieves us of excessive emotions that are harmful and painful. All these have an impact on our blood pressure, immune system, and risk of chronic illnesses. One study among high school students finds that "both materialism and compulsive buying have a negative impact on teenagers' happiness. The more materialistic they are and the more they engage in compulsive buying, the lower their happiness levels."

Jain Path

Fasting - Cultivating a mindset free from excessive attachment to food or desire for it, diminishing our preoccupation with consumption.

Food nourishes us, but it is also a tool for us to practice self-restraint and our spirituality. Fasting is a practice in nearly every faith, but it is highly emphasized in the Jain tradition. One can do a full day, half day with water or without, and then 8 days 10 days, or even 30-day fasts. Fasting is a spiritual activity.

Tattvartha Sutra 7.16/7.21 details "fasting on sacred days." More so in detail, "The sacred days for fasting are prescribed as the eighth, fourteenth or fifteenth day of the fortnight." Also Sutra 9.19 details, "The six external austerities are: fasting, semi-fasting or reduced diet, voluntarily limiting the variety and the manner of seeking food, giving up delicacies or a stimulating diet..."

During the days of Parushan Parv, Jains, young and old, practice fasting. Fasting has many health benefits. It promotes blood sugar control by reducing insulin resistance, reduces inflammation, and may impact blood pressure and cholesterol levels. Fasting helps to reduce obesity and, most importantly, builds one's willpower.

Austerities - Practicing moderation and restraint in our engagement with the five senses, while engaging in tap/tayag.

Our five senses provide pleasure and pain. Though we may enjoy the moments of pleasure, we also must bear the bouts of pain. Jain religion encourages the practice of austerities or self-restraint. If we have the ability to control the senses at our will, we can modulate the pain and be tempered during moments of pleasure. The practice of *Tap* (austerity) and *tyag* (letting go or detachment) also allows us to practice austerities in our daily lives. Fasting is one form of austerity, yet other practices include limiting our mobility. In today's world, limiting our use of technology and social media is a form of austerity.

In Tattvartha Sutra 9.6, among the 10 dharmas, the 6th and 7th are self-restraint and austerity, which are forms of penance. "Self-restraint refers to abstaining from all activities which injure any form of life, subtle or gross.... Controlling body, speech and mind."

Austerity is putting hardship on the body to regenerate the soul. There are many austerities, and the strictest ones apply to monks and nuns.

The health benefits of controlling our senses are essential life skills. We can control the mind in the face of physical and mental adversity. Austerity builds resilience. For one who has practiced austerities, any level of heat or cold, hunger or thirst, pain or suffering does not affect them. Austerity is a life-coping and survival skill. It rewires our brains to withstand any adversity.

Jain Path

Controlling Sensual Desires (*Sanyam* संयम) - Exercising self-control and detachment from excessive longing for sensual pleasures, as reflected in Sanyam संयम.

Sensual desires refer to those from the senses, such as the excessive desire for taste or for smell, but also that of sexual desires, which in form is the sensation of touch. While monks are celibate, laypersons live a life where they balance sensual desires.

Tattvartha Sutra 7.11/7.16 is touching when charged with lust. This refers to "free sexual activity outside of marriage." Other verses 7.23/7.27 detail the ill effect as transgressions "matchmaking, promiscuity, sex with whores, unnatural sexual practices, and intense sexual passions."

Also, among the 5 *anuvratas* the last Brahmacharya relates to excessive sensual desires, which in strictest form is celibacy.

The benefit of controlling excessive sensual desires is good moral conduct in society. Excessive sexual desire can lead to sexual misconduct and harm to others. The practice of Controlling Sensual Desires leads to living a balanced life and maintaining good relationships in the family.

Art of Dying - Embracing a state of detachment and non-attachment to both the material world and the body.

Letting go of material possessions may be easy, but letting go of family and friends and our own bodies at the end of life is difficult. The Jain principle of *Aparigraha* allows us to learn how to let go. Dying is the ultimate and final detachment, and there is an art to this.

The Tattvartha Sutra talks of detaching from the body in a methodical way.

Sutra 7.17/7.22 describes the detailed process of sallekhana, or holy death. When death is approaching, and one cannot continue with religious vows, then one can use a series of progressive fasts as a tool.

This is distinctly different from suicide, which is done out of anger, rage, and frustration. The holy death is deliberate and calculated and done after permission from a monk.

A proper mental attitude and a structured process of dying are essential in today's world. With ventilators to keep the lungs breathing and pacemakers and ECMO to keep the heart and blood pumping, it is often unclear when a person is alive or dead. Medicine today has new specialties, palliative care, and hospice care, which ease the dying process. Such specialties provide guidance that aligns with Jain practices. The Jain art of dying encourages making a resolution and getting approval, detaching from the material world through fasting, saying goodbyes to family members, and dying with contentment and peace. Such is a good death.

Charity (*Dana* दान) - Generously sharing one's wealth with others, free from attachment to money.

Donations can be with money or time. Time donation is service, and money donation is charity. It is not a matter of how much one gives but the intention of giving. The intention behind the charity is crucial. If one wishes for name recognition and fame from charitable contributions, it is not charity it is payment for self-interest and self-promotion.

Tattavartha Sutra 6.13/6.12 talks of charity giving to overcome inequity in the world: "Compassion through charity for all living beings." Also, Charity benefits the self with a sense of gratitude. Tattvartha Sutra 7.33/7.38 states, "Charity consists in offering alms to the qualified person for one's own benefit."

The health benefits of those who give to charity are well known through multiple studies. According to a Cleveland Clinic article, giving leads to lower blood pressure, less depression, less stress level, higher self-esteem, and greater happiness and satisfaction. According to one study, those "who were 55 years and older who volunteered for two or more organizations were 44% less likely to die over a five-year period than those who didn't volunteer."

Environmentalism - Embracing responsible resource usage and demonstrating care and respect for the Earth while refraining from personal possession of materials.

We need to save the earth and all living creatures and nonliving for future generations. Jain principle of *Aparigraha* promotes the idea of limiting waste and avoiding the unnecessary use of natural resources.

While environmentalism may seem to be a national or global problem, it begins with the individual. Jains, by nature, are ecologically conscious, yet they need to support international climate change accords. Encourage and vote for leaders who promote this agenda. Reducing cattle production for meat will reduce the greenhouse effect in reducing methane in the environment.

Tattvartha Sutra 7.16/7.21 states, "refraining from wanton destruction of the environment by thought, word and deed." Scriptures define wanton destruction of 5 types, including torturing animals and "negligent conduct such as recklessly cutting trees, digging or flooding fields, supplying lethal weapons." 7.27 states, "Limit Consumer Goods."

The health benefits of environmentalism are many, such as less pollution. For example, the pollution in large cities like New Delhi is equal to that of smoking one pack of cigarettes per day. The benefit of Environmentalism to the Earth is in reducing the carbon footprint and climate change.

HASSE (हँसी)
(Laugh in Hindi)

Health

Affection

Security

Significance

Equanimity

HASSE - THE ELEMENTS OF HAPPINESS

The aspiration in Jainism is to attain happiness in both our current existence and in our eternal journey. In daily life, Present Happiness is experienced through simple pleasures like relishing a delicious meal or earning recognition. Lasting Happiness, existing over the course of years and decades, is characterized by contentment and equanimity, such as in meditative states or detaching from material attachments. Eternal Happiness, extending beyond lifetimes, encompasses the sublime feelings of bliss and self-transcendence.

Although these happiness categories are not explicitly detailed in the scriptures, they are derived from the *Tattvartha Sutra* and hold relevance in the modern lives of laypersons.

To better understand the elements of happiness and Jain practices that lead to happiness, it is helpful to compare different philosophies. The great Greek philosopher Aristotle said, "Happiness is the meaning and the purpose of life, the whole aim and end of human existence… Happiness depends upon ourselves."

He described four levels of happiness.
Aristotle's Happiness Level 1- Laetus: Happiness from material objects. This leads to sensual pleasure and is short-lived. At a time of crisis this happiness becomes shallow and without meaning.
Aristotle's Happiness Level 2 - Felix or Ego gratification: Happiness from admiration from others. This happiness is unstable because failure is bound to happen and will lead to frustration. Also, self-promotion will lead to alienation from others.
Aristotle's Happiness Level 3 - Beatitudo or doing good: Happiness from doing good for others leads to connection, compassion, and friendship. This happiness is more lasting, yet even relationships are imperfect and lead to disappointment.
Aristotle's Happiness Level 4 - Sublime Beatitude or ultimate/perfect happiness. This happiness is connected with the universe in self-transcendence through religion or spirituality.

We can see there is tremendous overlap between Aristotle's four levels of happiness and the Present, Lasting, and Eternal Happiness that has been described on the Jain Path.

While achieving the pinnacle of Eternal Happiness or moksha may be beyond the reach of a layperson in the present life, seeking and nurturing Present and Lasting Happiness becomes paramount for a fulfilling journey.

So, how does one achieve Present and Lasting Happiness by following the Jain Path? The process of achieving this happiness is quite simple, but it is essential to understand the core elements of what makes us happy. These elements can be recalled using the acronym HASSE, which translates from Hindi to English as "laughter." Each letter represents an important component:

H is for Health - Consider the significance of good health as a source of happiness by asking a patient diagnosed with metastatic cancer undergoing chemotherapy.

A is for Affection - Reflect on the importance of affection by questioning someone experiencing a broken marriage.

S is for Security - Recognize the value of financial security by speaking to a father living in poverty who cannot provide the next meal for his children.

S is for Significance - Understand the need for a sense of purpose in life by conversing with empty nesters who feel lonely and without clear objectives.

E for Equanimity - Acknowledge the necessity of equanimity by listening to the experiences of a young woman whose emotions fluctuate between anger and exaltation.

These elements form the foundational pillars of happiness, and the lack of any of them can be the root cause of our unhappiness. Identifying which of these elements is lacking in our lives is the first step towards a path to a happier existence. Once we recognize the missing component, we can work towards fostering it through Jain practices and ultimately paving the way for a more joyful and fulfilling life. Below are the five elements of Happiness and a brief story derived from an AI Chatbot to help us remember the elements.

HASSE - The Elements of Happiness

At present, how happy are you in these domains: HASSE: Health, Affection, Security, Significance, Equanimity - On a scale of 1 to 5 - circle the answer.

Health ? / स्वास्थ्य ?		1 Not at all	2 Minimal	3 Somewhat	4 High	5 Complete
Affection ? / स्नेह ?		1 Not at all	2 Minimal	3 Somewhat	4 High	5 Complete
Security ? / सुरक्षा ?		1 Not at all	2 Minimal	3 Somewhat	4 High	5 Complete
Significance? / महत्व ?		1 Not at all	2 Minimal	3 Somewhat	4 High	5 Complete
Equanimity ? / समभाव ?		1 Not at all	2 Minimal	3 Somewhat	4 High	5 Complete

Calculate your Happiness Score

_____ x 4 = _____ **Happiness score**   www.JainPath.org
(Add all numbers above)   (out of 100)

Vegetarian/
Vegan/Jain Diet

Stress Free

Yoga and
Exercise

Fasting

Health
Well being
(healthy diet, exercise,
restful sleep)

Health

Health is physical well-being. We can achieve a healthy body with a healthy diet, regular exercise, and restful sleep. Jain practices that support a healthy body are vegetarian/vegan/Jain diet, stress-free lifestyle, regular exercise or yoga, and fasting.

> In a bustling city, there lived a young woman named Lata. She found herself juggling multiple responsibilities, leaving little time for self-care. Stress and fatigue became her constant companions as her health began to suffer. Alarmed, Lata decided to make a change. She prioritized a vegan diet, incorporating colorful fruits and vegetables into her meals. She embraced regular exercise, immersing herself in invigorating workouts. And she cherished the value of quality sleep, creating a peaceful bedtime routine.
>
> Gradually, the transformation unfolded. Lata regained her energy, her outlook brightened, and her body grew stronger. It was then she realized that diet, exercise, and sleep were not mere habits but essential pillars of a happy, healthy life.

Forgiveness

Carefulness

Compassion

Controling Sensual Desires

Affection
Emotional well being
(love, caring, managing stress, anger, greed, ego, deceit, etc.)

Affection

Affection is emotional well-being. It is love, caring, and connectedness. Affection finds its constraints within anger, ego, deceit, and greed. Of the 24 Jain practices, the four practices of forgiveness, carefulness, compassion, and controlling sensual desires lead to greater happiness. A story may help us better ingrain this element of happiness.

> In a quaint town, Sita and Shan epitomized the significance of affection in their relationship. Amidst life's trials, they nurtured their connection through small gestures of love—a comforting touch, heartfelt compliments, and words of appreciation. Their affection became a healing balm, easing wounds and strengthening their bond. They listened without judgment and supported each other's dreams. Through the ups and downs, their unconditional love served as a guiding light, bringing happiness to their lives.
>
> Their story reminded others that affectionate relationships hold the power to cultivate joy, acceptance, and a shared sense of belonging—a testament to the profound influence of love in achieving lasting happiness.

- Austerities 
- Intoxicant Free 
- Balancing Needs and Wants 
- Straight-Forwardness

Security
(physical, financial, relationship)

Security

Security relates to physical security (feeling safe in your neighborhood), financial security (having enough money for education or retirement), and relationship security (knowing that family or friends will care for you). We can achieve security through the good company of friends and neighbors, through education and a good job, and spending time with and listening to family and loved ones. The Jain practices of Austerities, Intoxicant free, Balancing Needs and Wants, and Straightforwardness can help with achieving happiness on the element of security.

> In a bustling city, Ekta strived for happiness. She realized that true contentment lies in the embrace of physical, financial, and relationship security. Ensuring her physical safety, she joined self-defense classes and practiced mindfulness while navigating her surroundings. Financial security came by saving diligently, investing wisely, and living within her means. Cultivating healthy relationships, Ekta maintained open communication, offered support, and sought understanding. The synergy of these securities created a harmonious foundation. Ekta emerged empowered, free from fear and uncertainty. With a sense of physical safety, monetary stability, and loving connections, she basked in the genuine happiness that sprouted from the fortification of her life on multiple fronts.

Environmentalism

Charity

Service

Equity

Significance
(social, compassion, community)

Significance

Significance is having a sense of purpose, social responsibility, and community commitment. We can achieve significance in our lives by taking on projects that will benefit others and provide satisfaction. The Jain practices of Service, Equity, Charity, and Environmentalism lead to great happiness in the element of significance.

An elderly man named Tanuj lived in a distant town. Often, he was alone, lost, and unfulfilled. His days blended into an indistinct blur, lacking purpose and meaning. Determined to break free from this aimless existence, encouraged by his daughter, he sought to find significance. Tanuj volunteered at Red Cross charities, helping to recruit blood donors. As he made a positive impact, he discovered a sense of purpose that stirred him deep inside. Through his actions, he realized that meaningful connections and making a difference brought him immeasurable happiness. Tanuj's journey taught him that finding significance is the key to unlocking a life filled with joy, fulfillment, and a true sense of purpose.

- Art of dying
- Scripture Reading
- Contentment
- Meditation and Mindfulness

Equanimity
(contentment, peace, harmony)

Equanimity

Equanimity is calmness and inner balance without agitation in the face of adversity. We can achieve equanimity in our lives through contentment, peace, harmony, and tranquility. The Jain practices of contentment, scripture reading, the art of dying, and meditation/mindfulness can help us achieve happiness on the element of equanimity.

> In a big city, which is often brimming with chaos and constant demands, lived a young woman, Seema. She was often driven by her emotions, swinging between anger and exuberance and feeling overwhelmed by life's ups and downs. She sought tranquility. So Seema embarked on a journey. Through meditation and mindful practices, she learned to observe her thoughts and emotions without judgment. As she embraced the calm within, Seema discovered inner peace and a newfound balance. No longer controlled by external circumstances, she navigated life's challenges with grace. Equanimity became her anchor, allowing her to find serenity amidst the storms and thus unlocking true happiness within.
>
> The 24 Jain practices can help to bring the five elements of happiness: HASSE - health, affection, security, significance, and equanimity into our daily lives.

JAIN PATH

Moksha / EQUANIMITY / Happiness

JAIN PRACTICES

JAIN WAY OF LIFE — *Right Faith-Knowledge-Conduct*

JAIN PRINCIPLES
- AHIMSA
- ANEKANTAVADA
- APARIGRAHA

JAIN PHILOSOPHY
- Theory of Life
- Theory of Soul
- Theory of Moksha
- Theory of Karma

Jain Practices / Way of Life:

- Intoxicant Free
- Compassion
- Vegetarian/Vegan/Jain Diet
- Forgiveness
- Yoga and Exercise
- Stress Free
- Service
- Carefulness
- Open-Mindedness
- Straight-forwardness
- Meditation and Mindfulness
- Scripture Reading
- Humility
- Equity
- Respect
- Prayer-Pooja
- Austerities
- Charity
- Fasting
- Balancing Needs and Wants
- Contentment
- Controlling Sensual Desires
- Art of Dying
- Environmentalism

CONCLUSION

The Jain Path is the philosophical construct for a Jain Way of Life. The Jain Path encapsulates the profound wisdom accumulated over thousands of years and distills it into a comprehensive framework comprising the 3 P's (Philosophy, Principles, Practices), the 3 A's (Ahimsa, Anekantavada, *Aparigraha*), the 4 T's (Theory of Life, Soul, Karma, Moksha), and 24 Practices. While some may view this as an oversimplification of the vast knowledge present in Jaina scriptures, it serves as a valuable primer on Jainism for many. Through this condensed framework, individuals can navigate the intricate depths of Jain philosophy and spirituality, gaining insights into the fundamental principles and practices that guide the Jain Way of Life.

Living according to the Jain Way of Life calls for steadfast adherence to the core principles of Ahimsa, *Anekantavada*, and *Aparigraha* and their application in our daily lives. By embracing these foundational principles and incorporating them into our actions, we honor the essence of Jain teachings and contribute to a more harmonious and compassionate existence. In this context, the Tattvartha Sutra emerges as the fundamental underpinning of Jainism, providing invaluable guidance and direction for those on the path of Jain philosophy and spirituality.

It is imperative for the evolution of Jainism to preserve its timeless philosophy and principles while interpreting its scriptures in the context of modern perspectives and outlooks. Religion is not static; rather, it is a dynamic force that should permeate our daily lives, serving as a source of inspiration and guidance. By delving deep into the wisdom of Jain teachings and understanding their practical relevance in contemporary society, we can embark on a journey of personal and spiritual growth. Embracing this deep evaluation of our beliefs and practices empowers us to integrate Jain principles into our daily lives, paving the way for the creation of our own unique path to happiness and fulfillment.

Ahimsa Practices and Tattvartha Sutra Shlokas

Vegetarian-Vegan/Jain Diet
7.30/7.35 Eating animate food, eating things in contact with animate food, eating things mixed with animate food, eating half-cooked food are transgressions

Forgiveness
9.6 Description of 10 Dharmas: Morality is perfect forgiveness

Compassion
6.13/6.12 Compassion through charity for all living beings and purity (freedom from greed) cause the inflow of pleasure karma

Service
5.21 Souls render service to one another
6.23 Describes the 16 virtues of Jina Path Service to others including monks and nuns

Yoga and Exercise
6.1 The action of the body, the speech organ and the mind is called yoga(activity)
6.2 These three types of yoga cause vibration/throbbing in the space points of soul resulting in influx(asrava) i.e. incoming of Karmas

Carefulness
9.4 Guarding through body, speech and mind
9.5 To move carefully is to talk, speak, seek, calm, handle objects of daily use and dispose of excreta in correct manner

Intoxicant Free
7.30/7.35 Drinking alcohol is transgression and distracts us from the spiritual path

Stress Free
9.24 Focus on single object is meditation which leads to less stress.
9.31 to 9.34/9.30 to 9.33 Describes about getting rid of disagreeable objects, unhappy situations, unpleasant feelings and intense anxiety

Anekantavada Practices and Tattvartha Sutra Shlokas

Open Mindedness
1.33 A person must not have a deluded world view else they are like an insane person
1.34 Perspectives are many ranging from a common person's view to a deeply philosophical view

Meditation and Mindfulness
7.7 To transform oneself through self awareness and self-reflection
9.27 The concentration of thought on a single object by a person is meditation

Respect
9.20 The six internal austerities: austerities, reverence(humility) service, scriptural study, renunciation and meditation

Humility
6.23 Jina Path
9.27 Morality is perfect humility

Straight-Forwardness
6.22 Straight forwardness attract beneficial Karma
9.6 Morality is perfect straight forwardness

Scripture Reading
6.14/6.13 Scripture for right world view
6.23/6.24 Jina Path

Equity
7.1 Vows on equity of living beings, perspectives and basic needs

Prayer
6.23 Jina Path

Aparigraha Practices and Tattvartha Sutra Shlokas

Balancing Needs and Wants
7.4/(7.5 to 7.9) Avoid greed and anger
7.27 Limit excessive use of consumer goods
7.16 Supplemental vows

Contentment
7.12/7.17 Clinging is possessiveness.

Fasting
7.16 Seven supplementaries fasting on sacred days

Austerities
9.6 Means mortification of body for regeneration of soul

Controlling Sensual Desires
7.11 In appropriate touching
7.23 Promiscuity, unnatural sexual practices and intense sexual passion.
7.7 To avoid listening to lewd stories

Art of Dying
7.17 Fasting as process of Dying

Charity
6.13/6.12 Charity leads to flow of positive Karma
7.33/7.38 The benefit to giver of Charity

Environmentalism
7.16 Seven supplementries states refraining from wanton destruction of the environment by thought, word, or deed,
7.27 Limit consumer goods

SELECTED READINGS FROM TATTVARTHA SUTRA

By Umasvati and translated by Dr. Natmal Tatia: *"That Which is: Tattvartha Sutra -a Classic Jain Manual for Understanding the True Nature of Reality"*

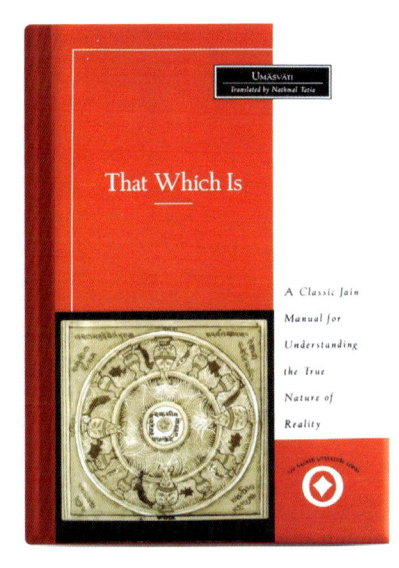

Tattvartha Sutra is a scripture written over 1,800 years ago. It has many truths to guide us. The sutras which are most relevant to modern life have been mentioned and commented upon here.

Also, the Jain practices that the sutras reveal are in color and underlines.

Translator's Introduction

The first paragraph of the translation by Dr. Nathmal Tatia is most valuable in setting the stage for the Jain Path.

The central themes of the Tattvartha Sutra are nonviolence, Nonabsolutism, and Nonpossessiveness. Nonviolence strengthens the autonomy of life of every being. Nonabsolutism strengthens the autonomy of thought of every individual. Non-possession strengthens the interdependence of all existence. If you feel that every soul is autonomous, you will never trample on its right to live. If you feel every person is a thinking person, you will not trample on his or her thoughts. If you feel that you own nothing and no one, you will not trample on the planet. In the second century CE, when the Jaina philosopher-monk Umasvati wrote the Tattvartha Sutra, these principles were the only way to global peace. Today, this is even more the case. These are the only values that can save humanity from the deadly acts of war, economic exploitation, and environmental destruction.

The format of commentary and sutras are in the following manner:

Sutra Number:
- → The first number is the Svopajna Bhasya version, which is followed by the Svetambara sect.
- → The second number followed by the "/" is *Saarvathasiddhi* version followed by the Digambara sect. Though nearly all the sutras are the same, the numbering differs in certain chapters.

Commentary is based on modern interpretation of the sutra.

The exact translation from *Tattvartha Sutra* is in bold and italics.

The color signifies which Jain Practice and Theory the sutras reveal.

Ahimsa practices are in blue.

Anekantavada **practices are in orange.**

Aparigraha **practices are in green.**

Chapter 1 - TRUTH

The Categories of Truth

The first chapter lays out the categories of truth that make up reality. **This chapter describes the Theory of Life.**

1.1 The Jain Path to liberation is defined. The right perception, right knowledge, and right conduct are the path to liberation
The enlightened word-view, enlightened knowledge, and enlightened conduct are the path to liberation.

1.4 The Nature of Reality exists in the categories of Truth. This sutra shows how Jains "frame" Reality and the universe. The fundamental distinction is between living and non-living.
The categories of truth are: 1. Soul 2. Non-sentient entities 3. The inflow of karmic particles to the soul 4. The binding of the karmic particle to the soul 5. Stopping the inflow of karmic particles 6. The falling away of the karmic particles 7. Liberation from worldly (karmic) bondage.

1.6 Categories are better understood by knowledge and the various philosophical standpoints. This sutra introduces the concept of multiple viewpoints or *Anekantavada*.
The categories can be understood with greater accuracy through the approved means of knowledge and the philosophical standpoints.

1.9 Knowledge or cognition is gained by the mind's ability to comprehend what is sensed. Varying types of knowledge are described.
The varieties of knowledge are empirical, articulate, clairvoyant, mind-reading, and omniscient knowledge.

1.33 The most critical element to the path to liberation is one's worldview. A worldview is determined by one's ethical and spiritual values. If the worldview is deluded, it will mislead thinking and conduct and take one on the wrong path. This sutra describes the *Anekantavada* practice of Open Mindedness.
A person with a deluded worldview is like an insane person who follows arbitrary whims and cannot distinguish true from false.

1.34 Conflicts arise when perspectives or viewpoints between individuals differ. Such conflicts occur due to philosophical standpoints. The Principle of *Anekantavada* is revealed when one looks at the world from varying viewpoints. This sutra describes the *Anekantavada* practice of Open Mindedness.
The philosophical standpoints are the common person's view, generic view, practical view, linear view, and literal view.

Chapter 2 - SOUL

The Nature of the Soul
The second chapter describes the nature of the soul, the types of soul, and its migration from body to body based on karma. This chapter describes the Theory of Soul

2.1 The uniqueness of the soul is discussed.
The states that distinguish the soul from other substances are those that: 1. Are due to the suppression of the deluding karma. 2. Are due to the elimination of the eight types of karma. 3. Are mixed because of the partial elimination and partial suppression of the four destructive karmas. 4. Are due to the rising of the eight types of karma 5. Constitute the innate nature of the soul.

2.8 Awareness or consciousness is the essential quality of the soul.
Sentience is the defining characteristic of the soul.

2.10 Souls are divided by those that are liberated (Arihant and Siddhas) and Worldly (all other beings).
The souls are divided into two broad classes: worldly beings and liberated souls.

2.11 Worldly souls are further divided into those that have a mind (humans) and those that don't (plants and animals).
The worldly souls fall into two groups: souls that possess a mind and souls that do not.

2.12 Souls are further divided by their ability of motion. Plants are immobile beings.
The worldly souls are further classified as mobile and immobile beings.

2.15 Some mobile beings have 5 senses.
There are five senses.

2.16-2.25/2.24 Senses are further defined as matter or as modes of the soul, which means they have the ability for awareness and perception.

2.26/2.25 Jainism believes in reincarnation and the migration of the soul to another life based on its karmas.
If the soul makes one or more turns when it is in transit after death, the only activity is that of its karmic body

2.42/2.41 The relationship between the soul and karma is defined here. Also, this sutra defines that man, woman or the soul were not created by any God.
And they (Karma) have been associated with the soul since beginningless time.

Chapter 3 - UNIVERSE

Jain Universe - Lower and Middle Regions

This chapter describes the various regions of the universe where the soul can take birth.

3.1 The creatures living in the lower region of the Jain Universe are described here. They are hellish creatures.
The infernal beings live in seven lands...

3.7 The distances, heights, and depths are described in detail, and names are given to islands and oceans. This was the prevailing understanding of the universe at the time of the writing of the Sutras.
There are islands and oceans that bear propitious names, such as Jammu Island, Lavanya Ocean, and so on.

3.27 Jain Time is cyclical and described in detail in this sutra.
During their time cycles of six ascending and six depending eons, the continents of Bharata and Airavata experience periods of prosperity and decline.

Chapter 4 - DEVAS

The Devas
Those living in the Upper Region of the Jain Universe are described here as Devas.

4.1 Types of Devas, as well as the characteristics and life span of Devas, are described in this chapter
The gods (Devas) fall into four classes.

4.2 -4.53 The sutras describe in detail the geography and lifespan of devas.

Chapter 5 - SUBSTANCES

Substances
Distinct from the soul are substances. The types, characteristics, and purpose of substances are described in this chapter.

5.1 The universe is divided by living (Jiv or that which has a soul) and nonliving (Ajiv - that which does not have a soul). The latter is described here.
The media of motion and of rest, space, and matter are extended non-sentient entities.

5.3/5.4 Substances also have no beginning or end. They are not created by a creator or God.
The substances are eternal, their number is fixed, and they are devoid of material attributes.

5.7 to 5.15 These Sutras describe the medium of motion and medium of rest, time, and soul and their units.

Jain Path

5.16 The relationship of the body and soul is much like that of the light of the lamp and the space it covers, clearly describing that the soul is both distinct and part of the body.
Like the light of a lamp, the soul assumes the size of the body happens to occupy on account of the contractions and expansion of its space units.

5.19 The function of matter is described in detail. It is to move the body.
Matter functions as the material cause of body, speech, mind, and breath.

5.20 Living beings are impacted by daily pleasure and pain. How pleasure and pain are produced is described. Matter, when it is nourishment such as food or water, sustains life, and matter, when it is a toxin such as poison, brings about death. Matter by itself does not cause pain or pleasure rather it is the karmas that are coming to fruition which cause the end result.
The production of pleasure, pain, life, and death is also due to matter.

5.21 This sutra is among the most well-known sutra of Jainism. It defines the relationship among souls all the while when individual souls are on an independent journey towards liberation. The function of the soul (favorable or unfavorable) is to serve one another. Souls cannot live independently of one another and share pleasure and pain with one another. Souls are partners in good and evil and are jointly responsible, even though the karmic result of actions is individual. The souls create a common environment. **This sutra describes the ahimsa practice of Service.**
Parasparopagrho Jivanam
Souls render service to one another.

5.22 Time as a substance is described.
The functions of time are becoming, change, motion, and the sequence of before and after.

5.25 Matter and its variety are described.
Matter has two varieties: atoms and clusters.

5.31/5.32 *Anekantavada*, though the word is not explicitly used in the *Tattvartha Sutra*, is described in the deep philosophical sense. Jainism subscribes to nonabsolutism. It denies absolute existence or absolute non-existence, absolute permanence or absolute impermanence. These sutras allude to the Doctrine of Nonabsolutism (*Anekantavada*), the Doctrine of Philosophical Standpoints, and Sevenfold Prediction (an investigation of the notions of existence, nonexistence, and inexpressibility attributed to reality).
The ungrasped (unnoticed) aspect of an object is attested by the grasped (noticed) one.

Chapter 6 - KARMIC FLOW

The inflow of Karma
The theory of Karma is critical to Jain Philosophy. Chapters 6, 8, and 9 detail this theory. **This chapter describes the Theory of Karma**.

6.1 Thought, Speech, and Action create activity, which is the vehicle for the interaction of the soul and the body with the universe. **The operation of the body, speech, and mind is action** (the word action here refers to activity while the word action in the sentence above refers to operation of the body).

6.3 The link between activity and karmic flow is made here. Also, activities are categorized as good and bad. Though this is a difficult moral judgment, e.g., is a cut from a surgeon's knife good or bad? The definition of good or bad largely depends on intentions. **Good actions cause the inflow of beneficial karma.**

6.4/6.3 Bad actions lead to bad karma.
Evil actions cause the inflow of harmful karma.

6.5/6.4 Passions are introduced as the caustic agents for the flow of karma. Any activity causes the flow of karma; however, less passionate activity leads to less bondage.
The activities of a person driven by passions cause long-term inflow (bondage), while the activities of a person free of passions cause instantaneous inflow (bondage).

6.6/6.5 Long term flow of passion is due to our five senses, four passions (anger, ego, deceit, and greed), five indulges (causing injury, lying, stealing, lack of self-restraint) and possessiveness, and 24 urges (e.g., malicious or murderous activity, disrespect of scriptures, damage of environment).
The different "doors" (causes) for the inflow of long-term karma are the five senses, four passions, five indulgences, and twenty-five urges.

6.7/6.6 The nature of bondage is determined by the intensity of passions, level of ignorance, and energy, as well as the instrument used.
The nature of karmic bondage caused by inflow varies according to the particular physical and psychological conditions of the subject. The conditions are high or low intensity of the passions, whether the act is done knowingly or unknowingly, the enthusiasm (energy) with which the act is done, and the instrument used in the act.

6.9/6.8 There are 108 permutations of the modes by which karma can bind to the soul. 3x3x3x4=108

Jain Path

The mode of the sentient instruments of inflow are the three stages of intention, preparations and commission; the three actions of body, speech, and mind; the three types of acts, those done by oneself, those in which one convinces others to undertake the act, and those undertaken by others but approved by oneself; and the for passions of anger, pride, deceit, and greed.

6.11/6.10 Karma's are of eight types. The knowledge covering and intuition covering karma are described here. **This sutra describes the *Anekantavada* practice of Scripture Reading.**
Slander, concealment, envy, obstructiveness, and disregard or condemnation of the scriptures, its keepers and instruments, cause the inflow of knowledge-covering and intuition-covering karma.

6.12/6.11 The intention and the action of causing pain attracts negative karmas. **This sutra describes the ahimsa practice of Compassion.**
Causing pain, grief, agony, crying, injury, or lamenting in oneself, or others, or both, attracts pain karma.

6.13/6.12
The intention and action of causing pleasure attracts positive karmas. Hence, all karmas are not bad. However, all karmas need to be relinquished in order to attain moksha. Similar to Bhagavad Gita 7.114, this is the reason for not harming animals and a vegetarian diet. **This sutra describes the ahimsa practice of Compassion.** This sutra describes the ***Aparigraha* practice of Contentment and Austerities and Charity.**
Compassion through charity for all living beings, especially those observing religious vows, the self-restraint of a person with attachment and the like, blameless activity, forbearance, and purity (freedom from greed) cause the inflow of pleasure karma.

6.14/6.13 Of the eight types of karmas, the cause of worldview deluding karma or not seeing the world from the perspective of the Jinas or religious order is described. **This sutra describes the *Anekantavada* practice of Scripture Reading.**
The inflow of view-deluding karma is caused by maligning the Jinas, their scripture, religion, order and doctrine, and the gods and goddesses.

6.15/6.14 Of the 8 types of karmas, the cause of conduct-deluding karma is passion.
The inflow of conduct-deluding karma is caused by the highly-strung state of the soul due to the rise of passions.

6.16 to 6.22 These Sutras describe how different types of activities lead to different situations as related to reincarnation.

6.23/6.24 This Sutra is important. It describes the 16 types of activities or virtues that lead to the path of Jina and salvation. **This sutra describes the ahimsa practice of Compassion and Service.** **This sutra describes the *Anekantavada* practice of**

Selected Readings From Tattvartha Sutra

Humility, Scripture Reading and Prayer Puja and Rituals. This sutra describes the *Aparigraha* practice of Contentment, Austerities and Charity.

The sixteen causes of body karma leading to the life of a Jina are: 1. purity of the worldview, 2. humility, 3. obeying the mores and abstinences, 4. persistent cultivation of knowledge, 5. dread of world existence 6. charity 7. austerity according to one's capacity 8. establishing harmony and peace in the monastic order 9. rendering service to the nuns and monks 10. pure devotion to the adorable one 11. pure devotion to the spiritual teacher 12. pure devotion to learned monks 13. pure devotion to the scripture 14. regard for compulsory duties 15. proper practice and promotion of the spiritual path 16. adoration of the learned ascetics in the scripture.

6.24/6.25 Flow of negative karmas occurs due to negative relationships and interaction with others. **This sutra describes the *Anekantavada* practice of Humility.**
Defaming others and praising oneself, hiding other's merits and finding fault, cause the inflow of karma leading to low status.

6.25/6.26 Flow of positive karmas occur due to positive relationships and interaction with others. **This sutra describes the *Anekantavada* practice of Humility.**
The opposites of the above causes, together with humility and modesty, cause the inflow of karma, leading to high status.

Chapter 7 - VOWS

Vows

The flow of various types of karmas is determined by vows. This chapter describes the vows or common practices one needs to follow to achieve salvation.

7.1 Ahima, *Anekandevada*, and *Aparigraha* (Nonviolence, Nonabsolutism, and Nonpossessivenes), the triple As's, are the core Jain Principles. They are described here as vows. This sutra is overarching for all the 24 practices. This sutra reflects the practice of equity, whereas nonviolence is equity of all living beings, nonabsolutism is equity of perspectives, and nonpossessiveness is equity of our basic needs.
Abstinence from violence, falsehood, stealing, carnality, and possessiveness - these are the vows.

7.3/7.4 To achieve the Triple A's, one requires a set of principles as described in this and the following sutras. **This sutra describes the ahimsa practice of Carefulness.**

Jain Path

Controlling speech, controlling the mind, moving about carefully, handling implements carefully, and inspecting food and drink properly to ensure they are acceptable.

7.4/(7.5 to 7.9) Sutras describe other practices such as giving up anger and greed or avoiding disputes, or avoiding explicit content that allows one to follow the vows. **These sutras describe the ahimsa practice of Forgiveness. This sutra describes the** *Anekantavada* **practice of Meditation and Mindfulness.** **This sutra describes the** *Aparigraha* **practice of Balancing Needs & Wants and Controlling Sensual Desires.**

7.5/7.10 The Universal source of suffering, the most painful aspect of existence, is caused by acts of violence. **This sutra describes the ahimsa practice of the Vegetarian-Vegan Diet.**
Acts of violence and so on are nothing but unmitigated suffering.

7.6/7.11 While the previous sutra talks about the negative aspect of Nonviolence, that is, not to do violence, this sutra talks about the positive aspect of nonviolence, which is to cultivate friendliness, compassion, and equanimity. **These sutras describe the ahimsa practice of Compassion.**
The observer of vows should cultivate friendliness towards all living beings, delight in the distinction and honor of others, compassion for miserable, lowly creatures, and equanimity towards the vainglorious.

7.7/7.12 How does one transform oneself to follow the vows? This sutra describes how to transform oneself through self-awareness and self-reflection. **This sutra describes the** *Anekantavada* **practice of Meditation and Mindfulness.** **This sutra describes the** *Aparigraha* **practice of Contentment.**
The observer of vows should reflect upon the nature of the world outside and inside his own body in order to quicken fear of, and disinterest in worldly life.

7.8/7.13 Violence is defined as taking life away due to passions of anger, ego, deceit, or greed. It is not the act of violence but rather the intention behind the violence. **This sutra describes the ahimsa practice of the Vegetarian-Vegan Diet.**
Taking life away out of passion is violence.

7.9/7.14 Other practices to avoid related to speaking falsehood, stealing, sexual misconduct, and obsessive attachment must be done with selfless intentions. **This sutra describes the** *Anekantavada* **practice of Straightforwardness.**
To speak what is not true is falsehood.

7.10/7.15 Stealing is a form of violence as well as greed.
Taking anything that is not given is stealing.

7.11/7.16 The desire or the act of touching another inappropriately or with lust leads to conduct deluding karma. **This sutra describes the *Aparigraha* practice of Controlling Sensual Desires.**
Coupling is carnality.

7.12/7.17 Attachment to material goods or even to the self is harmful. This sutra describes the Aparigraha practice of Contentment.
Clinging is possessiveness.

7.14/7.19 Vows are of two types. The very strict vows are for the monks, and the less strict vows are for the householder.
Observers of the vows fall into two classes: the householders and the homeless monks who have renounced violence and possessiveness.

7.16/7.21 To help with the vows there are supplemental vows related to the practices. **These sutras describe the ahimsa practice of Carefulness and Service. This sutra describes the *Aparigraha* practice of Balancing Needs & Wants, Fasting, and Environmentalism.**
The seven supplementaries that enrich the observer of the small vows are refraining from movement beyond a limited area, restricting movement to an even more limited area, refraining from wanton destruction of the environment by thought, word, or deed, keeping aloof from sinful conduct for a set period of time, fasting on sacred days and observing special restrictions at secluded places, limiting the use of consumables and non-consumable goods, offering alms to wandering ascetics.

7.17/7.22 This sutra provides the details of how a person goes through a spiritual death. **This sutra describes the *Aparigraha* practice of the Art of Dying.**
The householder should become a practitioner of the penitential rite of emaciation of the passions by a course of fasting, which spans a number of years and ends in death.

7.18 The limitation is our worldview or suspicion or doubt about a religious life, which is what holds us back from practicing these vows.
The transgressions of the enlightened worldview are suspicion, misguided inclination, doubt, praise for the heretical doctrines, and familiarity with the heretical doctrines.

7.21/7.26 The practice of Straightforwardness is a critical vow and is key to abstaining from falsehoods and deceit. **This sutra describes the *Anekantavada* practice of Straightforwardness.**
Wrong instruction, divulging secrets, forging documents, misappropriating funds, entrusted to one's care, and disclosing confidential deliberations.

Jain Path

7.22/7.27 Non-stealing is a practice given importance in the scriptures. Today, it relates to business and personal practices with deception, tax evasion, and fraud. **This sutra describes the anekantavada practice of Straightforwardness.**
Abetting theft, dealing in stolen goods, evading customs in foreign lands, misrepresenting the weight of goods one is buying or selling, and dealing in counterfeit goods.

7.23/7.28 Controlling excessive sensual desires is an important practice described in the sutra. **This sutra describes the *Aparigraha* practice of Controlling Sensual Desires.**
Matchmaking, promiscuity, sex with whores, unnatural sexual practices, and intense sexual passion.

7.27/7.32 This sutra describes untoward sexual comments or actions relating to sexual harassment as well as the overuse of products leading to environmental destruction. **This sutra describes the *Aparigraha* practice of Controlling Sensual Desires.**
Erotic talk, erotic gestures, garrulity, unmindful deeds beyond the set limit, and excessive use of consumer goods.

7.30/7.35 The vegetarian practice is clearly defined as a vow. The "animate food" refers to still living or living beings such as bacteria, flesh, and eggs. Also, drinking alcohol is a transgression and distracts us from the spiritual path. **These sutras describe the ahimsa practice of a Vegetarian/Vegan Diet and Intoxicant Free.**
Eating animate food, eating things in contact with animate food, eating things mixed with animate food, drinking alcohol, and eating half-cooked food.

7.33/7.38 Charity benefits the giver with a sense of gratitude. **This sutra describes the *Aparigraha* practice of Charity.**
Charity consists in offering alms to the qualified person for one's own benefit.

7.34/7.39 The value of a charity is dependent on many attributes ranging from the manner of giving to the conduct of the recipient. **This sutra describes the *Aparigraha* practice of Controlling Sensual Desires.**
The worth of a charitable act is determined by the manner of giving, the nature of the alms offered, the disposition of the giver, and the qualification of the recipient.

Chapter 8 - KARMIC BONDAGE

This chapter describes the Theory of Karma.

Karmic Bondage
After the inflow of karma, there is the binding of karma. The binding is dependent on a number of variables.

8.1 The sutra lays out the five causes of the bondage of karma. The causes related to 1. how we see the world, 2. if we indulge, 3. if we do not have enthusiasm for the beneficial karma, 4. if we have a passion such as anger, ego, deceit, and greed, and lastly, 5. all of the actions through our thoughts, speech, and action lead to the bondage of karma.

The five causes of bondage are deluded world-view, non-abstinence, laxity, passions and the actions of the body, speech, and mind.

8.4/8.3 This sutra now further defines the types of Bondage that relate to the type of karma, the duration of the bondage of that karma, the intensity by which the karma binds, and lastly, the quantity of the karma accumulated.

There are four aspects of bondage: type, duration, intensity (quality) of fruition, and mass of material particles assimilated.

8.5/8.4 In this sutra, the eight types of karmic bondages are described. Four types of bondages are related to the soul, and four relate to the body.

There are eight principal types of karmic bondage: knowledge-covering, intuition-covering, sensation, deluding, lifespan, body, status, and obstructive.

8.6 to 8.26 Details different types of karmas and how long the bondage they produce.

Chapter 9 - KARMIC INHIBITION

Inhibiting and Wearing Off Karma

This chapter describes how Karma can be inhibited. Often, the Jain practices help us with this. **This chapter describes the Theory of Karma.**

9.1 Karmas can flow in through "42 doors." Karmic inhibition can be mental or physical. Mental inhibition is when the mind and worldly action are disengaged. Physical inhibition is when the physical flow of karma stops due to this disengagement. The fourteen stages of spiritual development (*gunasthans*) are used to explain the stoppage of the inflow of karma. **This sutra describes the Theory of Karma**.

Stopping the inflow of karma is inhibition.

9.2 This sutra lays the broad outline of how to stop the inflow of karmas. This includes six ways, which are explained in great detail in the subsequent sutras one by one.

Inflow is inhibited by guarding, careful movement, morality, reflection, conquering hardships, and enlightened conducts.

9.3 In addition to the 6 ways, another way of inhibiting karmas is doing austerities as part of enlightened conduct. **This sutra describes the *Aparigraha* practices of Austerities.**
Austerities wear off karma as well as inhibiting it.

9.4 Being mindful or "guarding" one's actions, speech, and thoughts will inhibit karmas and is the first way of inhibiting karma. Mindfulness of actions means walking and moving carefully. Mindfulness of speech is religious discourse or even simple daily activities such as talking to the doctor or getting directions. Being silent is nobel. Mindful of thoughts means not having sinful intentions, reducing worldly thoughts, and engaging in spiritual thoughts. **This Sutra describes the ahimsa practice of Carefulness.**
Guarding is enlightened control of the threefold activities of body, speech, and mind.

9.5 Careful movement is much like mindful movement and the second way of inhibiting karma. While the sutra addresses mostly the movements of monks. The same practice applies to laypersons. **This sutra describes the ahimsa practice of Carefulness. This sutra describes the *Anekantavada* practice of Meditation and Mindfulness.**
To move carefully is to walk, speak, seek alms, handle objects of daily use, and dispose of excreta in the correct manner.

9.6 Ten moral values are described in this sutra. These moral values are the ten dharmas celebrated by the digambara Jains during the Daslakshan dharma at Paryushan Parv. **This sutra describes the ahimsa practice of Forgiveness, This sutra describes the *Anekantavada* practice of Open Mindedness, Humility, and Straight Forwardness. This sutra describes the *Aparigraha* practices of Austerities and Controlling Sensual Desires.**
Morality (moral values) is perfect forgiveness, perfect humility, perfect straightforwardness, perfect purity (freedom from greed), perfect truthfulness, perfect self-restraint, perfect austerity, perfect renunciation, perfect detachment, and perfect continence.

9.7 The fourth way of inhibiting the flow of karma is through the 12 reflections. These reflections allow one to realize the enlightened worldview or gain the Right Faith, *samyak darshan*. **This sutra describes the *Aparigraha* practices of Austerities and Fasting.**
The twelve reflections are upon impermanence, helplessness, the cycle of birth and death, solitariness, otherness of the body, impurity of the body, inflow of karma, inhibiting karma, wearing off karma, the nature of the cosmos, rarity of enlightenment and the lucid exposition of the doctrine.

9.8 The fifth way of inhibiting the flow of karmas is enduring hardships. There are 24 physical hardships and 14 spiritual development hardships which are all described later. **Enduring hardships prevents deviation from the spiritual path and wears off bound karma.**

Selected Readings From Tattvartha Sutra

9.9 Physical hardships relate to tolerating situations such as hot or cold, hunger or thirst, illness, loss of faith, and lack of intelligence. Exercising or physical ailment are forms of physical hardship that lead to inhibiting the inflow of karma. **This sutra describes the ahimsa practice of Yoga and Exercise. This sutra describes the *Aparigraha* practices of Austerities and Fasting.** *There are twenty-two hardships arising out of hunger, thirst, cold, heat, insect bites, nudity, ennui, women, travel, seat and posture of practicing austerities, sleeping place, indignations for reproach, injury caused by others, seeking alms, lack of gain, physical ailment, touch of thorny grass, dirt, honor and reward, learning, lack of intelligence, and loss of faith.*

9.10 to 9.18 Hardships also relate to spiritual development or the *Gunasthans*.

9.19 The seventh way of inhibiting the karmic inflow is through external austerities. **The sutra describes the *Aparigraha* practice of Fasting and Austerities.**
The six external austerities are fasting, semi-fasting or reduced diet, voluntarily limiting the variety and the manner of seeking food, giving up delicacies or a stimulating diet, lonely habitation, and mortification of the body.

9.20 The seventh way of inhibiting the karmic inflow also includes six internal austerities. **The sutra describes the *Aparigraha* practice of Austerities. The sutra describes the *Anekantavada* practice of Respect and Humility Meditation and Mindfulness, and Scripture Reading. The sutra describes the ahimsa practice of Service.**
The six internal austerities are: penance, reverence (humility) service, scriptural study, renunciation, and meditation.

9.21-9.26 Many types of internal austerities that relate to the Practice of Austerities and Service.

9.27 Meditation is described as a restful mind, not a restless mind. The restful mind concentrates on a single object. Also, meditation is a Stress-Free state where no negative karmas are flowing. **The sutra describes the ahimsa practice of Stress-Free. The sutra describes the *Anekantavada* practice of Meditation and Mindfulness.**
The concentration of thought on a single object by a person with good bone-joints is meditation.

9.28 Sutra describes meditative austerity. **The sutra describes the *Anekantavada* practice of Meditation and Mindfulness.**
The meditative state lasts an intra-hour (less than 48 minutes).

9.29 Sutra describes four types of meditations, which are varying types of thought processes. **The sutra describes the *Anekantavada* practice of Meditation and Mindfulness.**
There are four kinds of meditation: mournful, wrathful, analytic, and white (pure).

9.30/9.29 Worldly life is nourished by the first two types of meditations: mournful and wrathful, while the last two, analytic and pure meditation lead to liberation. **The sutra describes the *Anekantavada* practice of Meditation and Mindfulness.**
The last two kinds of meditation, analytical and white, lead to liberation.

9.31/9.30 Sutra describes mournful meditation, which creates stress and anxiety. **The sutra describes the ahimsa practice of Stress-Free. The sutra describes the *Anekantavada* practice of Meditation and Mindfulness.**
Swelling on ridding oneself of contact with disagreeable objects or getting out of an unhappy situation is mournful meditation.

9.32 Unpleasant feelings are also mournful meditation. **The sutra describes the ahimsa practice of Stress-Free.**
Dwelling on ridding oneself of unpleasant feelings is also a mournful meditation.

9.34/9.33 Intense anxiety is also mournful meditation. **The sutra describes the ahimsa practice of Stress-Free.**
Intense anxiety to fulfill unfulfilled desires in future lives is also mournful meditation.

9.36/9.37 Analytical meditation is focusing on scriptures, universal suffering, the fruition of karmas, and the structure of the universe. **The sutra describes the *Anekantavada* practice of Scripture Reading.**
Dwelling on investigating the essence of the scriptural commandments, the nature of physical and mental suffering, the effects of karma, and the shape of the universe and its contents is analytic meditation.

9.42 Pure meditation is the meditation most familiar in modern times and is of four varieties. The first Pure meditation relates to scriptural contemplations from different philosophical viewpoints (the beginning, the end, and the continuity) of different entities, such as the self. The second Pure meditation is focused attention or unitary contemplation, much like a flame in a room with no wind. The third Pure meditation is the moments before omniscience with only subtle movement of the body, such as respiration. The fourth Pure meditation is irreversible stillness and liberation. **The sutra describes the *Anekantavada* practice of Meditation and Mindfulness.**
The four varieties of white meditation are: multiple contemplation, unitary contemplation, subtle infallible physical activity, and irreversible stillness of the soul.

Chapter 10 - MOKSHA

Liberation

This chapter describes the Theory of Moksha.

10.1 When all the karmas are eliminated, then the soul achieves liberation or omniscience or "the perfectly pure, the enlightened one, the all-knowing, the all-intuiting, the victorious, the absolutely alone." This sutra describes the Theory of Moksha.
Omniscience arises when deluding karma is eliminated and, as a result, knowledge-covering, intuition-covering, and obstructive karma are eliminated.

10.2 In order to achieve liberation, no new karma is flowing and bonding.
There is no fresh bondage because the causes of bondage have been eliminated and all destructive karmas have worn off.

10.3/10.2 Liberation is defined with complete certainty.
The elimination of all types of karma is liberation.

TESTIMONIALS

"Jain Path beautifully distills the essence of Jainism. I found the 3A's (Ahimsa-Anekantavada-Apriagraha), 3 P's (Philosphy-Principles-Practices), 4 T's (Theory of Life-Soul-Karma-Moksha), and 24 Practices framework to be incredibly insightful."

Dr. Abhay Firodia - Firodia Institute of Philosophy History and Culture

"As a second-generation Jain youth in America, I am always seeking to understand the faith and how to better incorporate it in my life. The Jain Path book distills the essence of Jainism in a simple guide and contextualizes our philosophy and practice within the 21st century."

Anjali Doshi - Former Director of Education for Young Jains of America

"As a Jain practitioner, I found 'Jain Path' to be an invaluable resource. It offers a deep understanding of Jain philosophy and offers practical guidance on how to incorporate Jain principles into daily life. This book has enriched my spiritual journey."

Prem Jain - JAINA past president and former Senior Vice President at Cisco Systems

"Jainism has many scriptures and practices. Jain Path brings forward the most relevant philosophy, practices, and principles for our time."

Acharya Lokesh Muni - Founder President, Ahimsa Vishwa Bharti

"The Jain Path book is a roadmap to a fulfilling life. It beautifully encapsulates the core principles of Jainism, such as Ahimsa, Anekantavada, and *Aparigraha*, and translates them into actionable practices for today's world."

Ramesh Shah - Founder of Jain Foundation